Total Quality Improvement Guide for Institutions of Higher Education

by
Robert A. Cornesky
Samuel A. McCool

Magna Publications
Madison, Wisconsin

Library of Congress Cataloging-in-Publication Data

Cornesky, Robert.
    Total quality improvement guide for institutions of higher education / by Robert A. Cornesky
and Samuel A. McCool.
            p. cm.
    Includes bibliographical references.
    ISBN 0-912150-21-1
    1. Universities and colleges–United States–Administration. 2. Universities and colleges–
Administration–Statistical methods. 3. Total quality management–United States–Statistical methods.
4. Problem solving–Statistical methods.
    I. McCool, Samuel A. II. Title
    LB2341.c768   1992
    378.73–dc20   92-15863
                                                                                 CIP

Second Printing 1994

Printed in the United States of America

Library of Congress Catalog Card Number: 92-15863

Magna Publications, Inc.
2718 Dryden Drive
Madison, WI 53704-3086
(800) 433-0499
(608) 246-3580

Table of Contents

INTRODUCTION

A friend recently commented that stupidity is doing the same thing over and over again in exactly the same manner and expecting the results to be different. In many instances, however, this is precisely what we do while managing the "processes" and "systems" in our educational institutions. Total Quality Management (TQM), on the other hand, involves procedures where one constantly examines the way things are done and looks for ways to improve the "processes" and "systems" to obtain better results. The purpose of this book is to describe the steps and tools of TQM and their use in academic units for Total Quality Improvement (TQI). We provide case studies from various colleges and universities.

What is TQM? In a nutshell, it's a management-driven philosophy that encourages everyone in the organization to know the organizational mission and to adopt a quality philosophy to continuously improve on how the work is done to meet the satisfaction of the customer. The general principles of TQM encourage everyone in the organization to point out dysfunctional processes and systems and recommend improvements. For this to occur, management (administrators, etc.) must effectively cultivate the arts of listening, analyzing, and implementing. TQM encourages teamwork. It's not a set of inflexible rules and regulations.

Why should TQM be implemented? Because it will increase the quality of education as it decreases the cost of delivering education. In addition, it will increase the competitiveness of academic systems, improving their ability to meet the challenges of change that are probably most evident in the growing awareness of critical thinking, diverse student populations, and global issues. It will improve significantly the morale of most employees, regardless of their role in academia.

This book is divided into two sections. In the first section, we describe The Steps:

- How to identify problems contributing to non-value-added work,
- How to construct a team to work on the problems,
- How to analyze the root causes of the problems,
- How to implement the recommendations of an action team.

Although we use a case study from the School of Arts & Sciences at a state university as the primary example in this section, you can assume that similar problems will originate in any unit or division within an educational setting.

In the second section, we describe the tools that are useful for implementing TQI processes in an academic setting.

SECTION I: The Steps

CHAPTER 1: IDENTIFYING THE PROBLEM(S)

Sometimes it's obvious what the principal problems of a given academic unit are and why they need to be addressed. In most cases, however, a major "system" that inhibits quality within a unit may not be readily apparent, either to the administrator or to most of the members of the unit.

Some say their department or school has so many serious problems that they don't know where to begin. As a result, it's a common mistake among deans, directors, and chairs to draw up meaningless long-range plans in an attempt to identify and correct all of the problems in three to five years. The objectives of the plan cannot be met because resources cannot be diverted from the "real" to the "ideal," and the faculty and staff who helped design the long-range plan become disenchanted when their proposed remedies are not implemented. Morale suffers, and the resulting inaction is viewed as "business as usual."

In order to concentrate on the major problems that prevent a unit from doing quality work, it may be necessary for deans, directors, and/or chairs to have each school or department identify the major problems by one or more of the tools listed in Figure 1.1. We explain the procedures for using TQI tools to attack these problems in Section II.

Using the Nominal Group Process (NGP) and several other tools mentioned below, the dean of the School of Arts & Sciences in our case study had his 10 department chairs identify and rank the major problems/processes that were perceived to inhibit quality. The results of the NGP are shown in Figure 1.2 on page 5.

Throughout the first section of this text, we'll follow the problem "**Insufficient Sections/Seats of General Education Classes**" to demonstrate how various TQI tools were used not only to solve this "systems" problem, but also to save several million dollars — as a result of improving the processes that contributed to this and others.

Between the NGP and other TQI analyses, the dean and faculty of the School of Arts & Sciences suggested to the academic vice president that she establish a cross-functional action team to concentrate on the registration "system." This was the event at which the crisis manifested itself; additional sections of general education courses were hastily added, and the class sizes were capriciously increased to meet the demand of incoming students. After consultation, the academic vice president appointed a cross-functional action team consisting of the registrar from the academic dean's office, the dean of the School of Arts & Sciences, two chairs from the school's academic departments, a faculty member from the School of Business, a faculty member from the School of Education, the associate director of the computer center, two maintenance personnel, a secretary, and the director of institutional research and planning.

The team met, and the academic vice president gave the members background information and the specific charge of finding out why the school always had to add additional sections of general education classes and raise the seat counts at every registration. In addition, the task force was charged with making specific recommendations to improve the registration system. The system to be analyzed was identified!

Figure 1.1
Total Quality Improvement tools

Affinity Diagram
- Used to examine complex and hard-to-understand problems
- Used to build team consensus
- Results can be further analyzed by a Relations Diagram

Cause and Effect Diagram (Fishbone)
- Used to identify root causes of a problem
- Used to draw out many ideas and/or opinions about the causes

Flow Charts
- Gives a picture of the process and the system

Force Field Analysis
- Used when changing the system might be difficult and complex

Histogram
- A bar graph that displays information about data set and shape
- Can be used to predict the stability in the system

Nominal Group Process
- A structured process to help groups make decisions
- Useful in choosing a problem to work on
- Used to build team consensus
- Used to draw out many ideas and opinions about the causes

Pareto Diagram
- Bar chart that ranks data by categories
- Used to show that a few items contribute greatly to the overall problem
- Helps the team identify which processes/systems to work on

Relations Diagram
- Helps the team analyze the cause and effect relationships between factors of a complex issue or problem
- Directs the team to the root causes of a problem

Systematic Diagram
- Used when a broad task or goal becomes the focus of the team's work
- Often used after an Affinity Diagram and/or Relations Diagram
- Used when the task is complex or when the action plan needed to accomplish the goal is complex

Figure 1.2
The ranks and final values of perceived
problems using the Nominal Group Process

Rank	Perceived Problem	Final Value
1	Insufficient Sections/Seats of General Education Classes	114
2	Large Class Sizes	66
3	Untimely Personnel Plan	42
4	Poor Budgeting Processes	36
5	Boss-Type Managers	13
6	Poor Students	13
7	Insufficient Laboratory Supplies	10
8	Not Enough Majors	4
9	Dirty Classrooms	2
	Total	300

Since classes have to be taught and other routine functions have to be performed, it is unreasonable to expect any institution of higher education or any academic unit to undertake a revamping of more than one or two major systems a year. In addition, as we will demonstrate in the remaining chapters, most systems and their processes are interrelated, sometimes in very remote ways.

The dean of the School of Arts & Sciences described above came on board as the registration process was occurring. As a result, the major issue he had to address was adding sections of courses and increasing class sizes to meet the demand of incoming students. Meanwhile, the faculty were irate, and rightly so. Instead of responding to emotional outcries, the new dean conducted an NGP and introduced the department chair to several TQI tools. The dean wanted to specifically identify and obtain group consensus on the major system that had to be improved, so that the faculty would maintain quality educational experiences and have greater pride in their work.

It is entirely possible that the ranking of the perceived problems could have been different if the dean had arrived during the submission of the annual personnel plan or during the budgeting process. However, as will become evident later, TQI procedures addressing either of these systems probably would have identified similar root causes to the overall institutional inefficiencies.

CHAPTER 2: FORMING THE ACTION TEAM

There is nothing more important in building a positive work climate than having cooperative teams. Teamwork makes it possible for an institution with average employees to transform the organization into one of high quality. Teamwork makes all people within the organization feel responsible for the organization; as a result, they will cooperate in creating a positive culture where working is fun and morale is high. Moreover, teamwork involves the members in collaborative work that not only helps to reinforce the mission of the team for the individual members, but models a pattern of learning behavior appropriate to an academic community.

Once a top-priority project is identified, management should appoint either a functional or a cross-functional action team. A functional team consists of people working within the same unit while a cross-functional action team consists of people from different units who are part of the "system" that needs "repair." In the previous chapter's example, the academic vice president included not only faculty and administrators on the team to examine the university's cumbersome registration process, but also several maintenance personnel, the associate director of the computer center, a department secretary, and others.

The maintenance personnel were selected because they had to set up the auditorium with desks, computers, and partitions before each registration. In the end, the maintenance personnel suggested renovations to the auditorium to make the flow of students become more efficient.

The associate director of the computer center made several suggestions that permitted improved scheduling and billing processes. As a result, several "hassle" factors of registering at the university were eliminated.

The department secretary, who was pulled from her regular job during registration, was responsible for supervising the secretaries who operated the computer terminals and entered the student's schedules into databases. She suggested that several additional screens be made available to the secretaries and to the students. She also suggested the installation of telephones at strategic places so that secretaries and students could contact advisors and/or department chairs as problems came up.

The result of implementing the cross-functional team's recommendations: the number of complaints dropped from over 500 per registration to fewer than 25!

Although participation on a team should be voluntary, proper teaming is important for the successful implementation of TQI. Once a team is formed, however, management must give it the proper support and recognition. Otherwise, morale will deteriorate.

According to Waterman's *Adhocracy: The Power to Change* (p. 23), the team leader ". . . should not be the expert in the area being studied or a member of the top executive ranks." If so, groups tend to defer to the person with the expertise or power.

Of course there are those occasions in which it is obvious who the team members should be. For example, if the problem being addressed is unique to an academic department, most likely the team members should consist solely of department members.

In most cases, however, a "system" problem usually affects more than one unit. For example, ordering supplies for a course in the biology department may involve a faculty member, the department secretary, and personnel from purchasing, receiving, and the business office. If receiving the supplies in a timely fashion is a major problem, a cross-functional team should consist of members from each of the units involved.

Usually it's desirable to examine a problem from many perspectives. Issues such as cultural diversity, political correctness and ethics, teaching and learning styles, and student assessment — to name just a few — have become major topics of discussion at colleges and universities. Appointing a cross-functional team to address one of these issues may require a tool like the Myers-Briggs personality test to ensure team diversity.

Depending on the institution and the magnitude of the project, it may be necessary to assign one or more full-time staff to the project. In addition to a top manager, whose main duties are to act as a facilitator and to listen carefully to reports, the team should be given the resources (e.g., secretary, room, word processor, computer terminal, reports, data) to do the job. This effort tells the organization that this project and this team are important!

After the team is formed, a top administrator should address the group at the first meeting. She or he should spell out the problem to be addressed and assure the group that they will be given the support necessary to investigate the problem. The team should be given a timeline that includes a date when verbal progress reports are to be delivered to the top administrator. (This is why top administration must become knowledgeable about TQM/TQI tools and techniques.) The team should be informed that all data necessary to investigate the project will be available for its examination. In other words, a feeling that nothing is sacred should be established. It is also a good idea for the top administrator to periodically attend team meetings to emphasize the importance of the project.

As mentioned in the previous chapter, no academic department, school, or institution should undertake more than two major projects a year. This is especially important if your team members have no training in TQI and in the use of TQI tools. In addition, it is very possible that several "task forces," either unit-specific or cross-functional, will have to be appointed to assist the action team in:

- Further defining the system under study,
- Assessing the current system,
- Analyzing the causes of poor processes,
- Improving the processes,
- Implementing and standardizing the improvements.

CHAPTER 3: ANALYZING THE CAUSES

Before a TQI action team can offer suggestions on how a "system" should be improved, it has to assess the current situation and analyze the causes for the system not performing up to expectations. For example, the top-ranked problem of not having enough sections of general education courses would appear to lend itself to an immediate solution, namely, hiring additional faculty. Other possible solutions might include adding sections of general education courses or increasing class sizes in general education courses at the onset of the scheduling process. However, as we will see, the root causes of the problem would not have been discovered if such "quick fix" approaches were taken.

Many of the TQI techniques of value in academic settings concentrate on the "process" approach, in which people work on the processes and/or tasks that make up a system. In this approach, one assumes that people want to do a quality job and that the major inhibiting factors are the poor systems in which they work. Furthermore, management must accept the fact that 85-95% of the systems in which faculty and staff perform their duties are under the control of management. As a result, management must admit that it might be the major cause of poor institutional quality and understand the root causes of problems within a system.

In order to understand the system under investigation, the action team has to analyze the processes. In addition to the TQI tools listed in Figure 1.1, action teams may find the tools listed in Figure 3.1 to be of value in assessing and analyzing the causes of problems within systems.

With this in mind, let's analyze the approach taken by the cross-functional action team as it examined the problems associated with the **registration system**.

Before working on the various processes making up the system, a team should describe the nature of the system, including its customers, purpose, output, required resources, and sources of input. In this case, the team designated the registration system as having the students and the faculty as its customers. (Each is a "customer" in the sense that each is an "end-user" of the product of the registration system — students because they register in various course offerings, and faculty because they fill class slots the registration system produces.) The registration system's purpose was to provide each student the opportunity to register for the classes required for graduation in a timely manner. The output of the registration system was to provide schedules to students and faculty, as well as to the personnel in ancillary services such as the scheduling office and bookstore, so that classrooms could be identified and materials could be ordered and available before the beginning of the first class.

In order to determine the number of courses and seats needed, accurate input data would be required from "feeder" systems, namely, the Recruiting & Admissions Office, the Office of Institutional Research & Planning, the school deans and their respective department chairs, and the dean who produced the final schedules.

With the system defined, the action team should write a project declaration and start gathering the necessary data. In the example case, the project declaration read: "It is the purpose of this action team to make specific recommendations to improve the registration system by scheduling the appropriate number of general education courses with reasonable class sizes to meet the demands of all students three months prior to the first day of scheduled classes."

Figure 3.1

Additional TQI tools that are useful in assessing
and analyzing system performance in academic units

Control Charts
- Used when system data are collected over time
- Used to measure stability and improvement of system
- Used to minimize chance of over- and/or under-controlling a system

Operational Definition
- Used to determine a definition of measure
- Used with all data
- Used to clarify and define quality measures for members of an action team

Run Chart
- Used when examining a system over time
- Used when an action team is gathering baseline data at the onset of analysis
- Used when either variable or attribute data are collected as function of time

Scatter Diagram
- Used to evaluate a relationship between two pieces of data

To demonstrate clearly the things that infringed upon the system and processes being studied, the action team drew a **Flow Chart** (see Section II). The action team took great pains to identify the system it was working on by including a beginning and an ending point, as well as those "systems" that contributed data and/or decisions that would have an impact on the registration system. The flow chart is shown in Figure 3.2 on the next page.

Figure 3.2
Interaction between the "systems" that produce
a schedule and register students

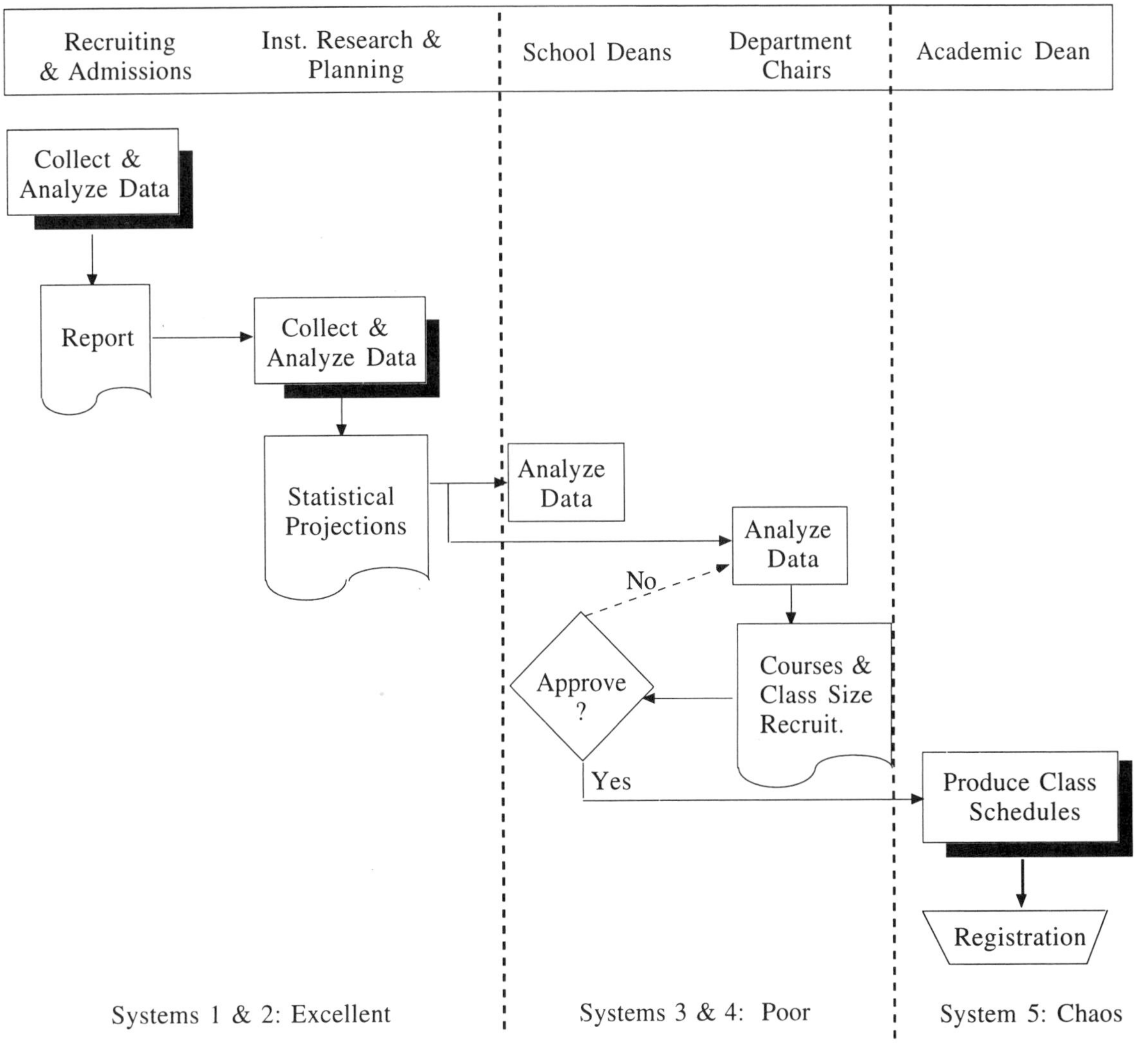

Recruiting & Admissions	Inst. Research & Planning	School Deans	Department Chairs	Academic Dean

Collect & Analyze Data

Report → Collect & Analyze Data

Statistical Projections → Analyze Data

Analyze Data

No - - - Approve ?

Courses & Class Size Recruit.

Yes → Produce Class Schedules

Registration

Systems 1 & 2: Excellent   Systems 3 & 4: Poor   System 5: Chaos

Having identified the system, the team decided to evaluate the registration data over the past three years. Data were readily available on a number of general education courses and the additional seats that had to be added. The team discovered the following:

- Based on statistical trends and information received from the Recruiting & Admissions Office, the Office of Institutional Research & Planning predicted with extreme accuracy the number of courses and seats that should be offered for students to meet general education requirements. The office also predicted with great accuracy which courses would be in highest demand. The office submitted its projections to the three school deans and to the department chairs almost nine months before registration. There was no doubt that the systems in Recruiting & Admissions and Institutional Research & Planning were meeting the time and accuracy requirements for the registration process.

- The approved class schedules submitted by the three deans did not meet the needs as projected by Institutional Research & Planning. Apparently, the deans did not communicate. As a result, the schedules exacerbated the problem. Although each schedule was lacking the appropriate number of general education courses, each was submitted at least eight months before registration. It was obvious that the **registration system** problem began at the school level — but why wasn't it corrected?

- The input to the academic dean from the school deans was inaccurate and contributed to the problem. But the number of errors in the final schedule could not be attributed to the simple accumulation of errors on forms submitted by the school deans. Something else was wrong.

The team decided to begin its investigation at the school level. It posted **Cause and Effect** diagrams (see Section II) in each school. The problem for which the team requested input from faculty was, "Why Didn't the School Schedule Enough General Education Courses?" After several weeks, the diagrams were collected and the results were compiled (see Figure 3.3 on the next page).

Figure 3.3

An Ishikawa (Cause and Effect) diagram showing the perceptions of the faculty
in the School of Arts and Sciences as to why an insufficient
number of general education courses were scheduled

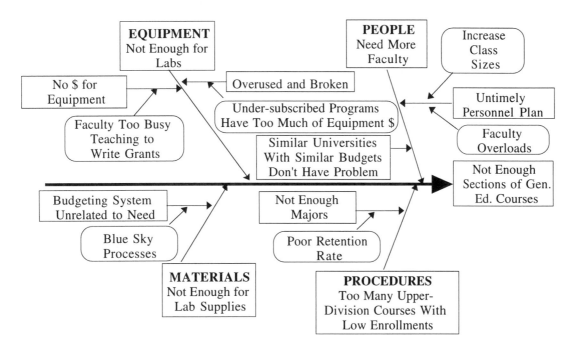

People Category

While the action team was waiting for the results of the **Cause and Effect** diagram, it began to plot the number of general education courses that had to be added to registration, by semester and by school, over the past seven years — the period for which it had the data. It did the same for the number of seats that had to be added during registration. For this, it used several **Control Charts** as described in Section II. But it did not have the data necessary for statistical analysis. The charts did show, however, that the number of courses/seats added was high, and that it increased in each of the three schools as enrollment increased. In other words, the system appeared to be unstable.

When the action team members first examined the data from the **Cause and Effect** diagram, they were almost lulled into believing that the problem could be attributed solely to the **People Category**. They reasoned that there were not enough faculty to meet the curricular demands, for if there were, additional general education courses could be offered and class sizes could be reduced to a level where meaningful discussions and assessments could take place.

Even though the university had hired a large number of faculty over the previous three years, the departments had not gotten approval to begin the searches in a timely fashion. The academic vice president, it appeared, could not bring herself to make a timely decision. As a result, she and the president claimed the budget did not permit hiring the number of faculty that were being requested; thus, they had to prioritize the positions.

As a result of not having a timely personnel plan, the schools had to add courses on an overload basis and increase class sizes. These actions resulted in overworked faculty and poor educational experiences for students. What caused the team to examine the issue further was the observation posted by a school dean: "Similar Size Universities With Like Budgets Don't Have This Problem." After verifying the dean's note, the team agreed to examine the other three categories, namely **Equipment, Materials,** and **Procedures**.

Working with the school deans and the academic vice president, the team members constructed a **Flow Chart** of the **Hiring System**. The hiring system obviously included the creation of the personnel plan. The flow chart is shown in Figure 3.4 on the next page.

Figure 3.4
A flow chart of the hiring system at a comprehensive state university

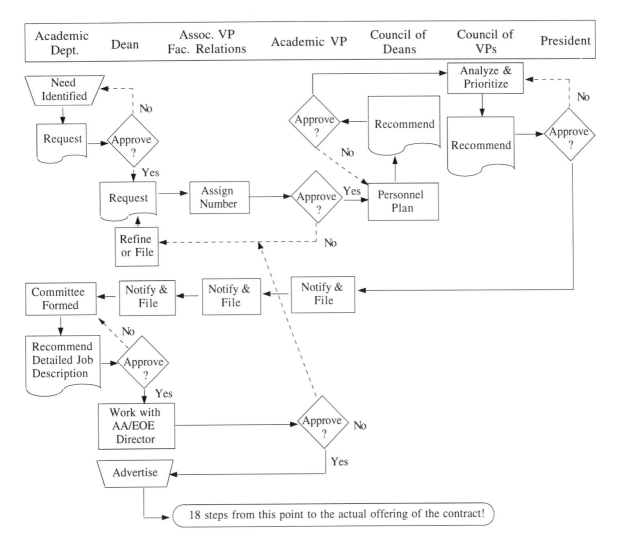

It became apparent that the bureaucratic system for hiring was out of control. In many instances, it took over 200 working days from the actual submission of a departmental request to the actual offering of a contract. The team concluded that the hiring system, which was under control of upper management, was obviously contributing to the problem increasing the number of sections and seats for general education courses.

With this information in hand, the Council of Deans and the academic vice president examined the **Hiring System**. After several months of using TQI methods, they received permission from the president to implement the **Revised Hiring System** as indicated in Figure 3.5 on the next page. Credit for improving the hiring system was given to the **Registration Action Team,** since it had they initially pointed out the problem.

Figure 3.5

A flow chart of the "revised hiring system" at a comprehensive state university

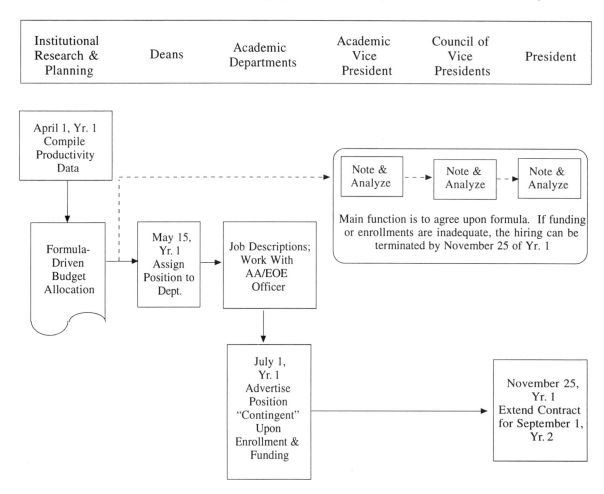

The new hiring system would assist in the employment of new faculty in a timely manner. The number of faculty would be determined statistically and would be driven by a predetermined allocation formula. The vice presidents felt comfortable with this decision, since the Office of Research & Planning and the Recruiting & Admissions Office had such stellar records in predicting enrollments. By being able to offer faculty contracts 10 months before the start of classes, the academic departments and school deans were able to approach new markets for the faculty. They could even consider people who were expecting to receive their Ph.D.'s in the summer before the start of classes in September! In addition, if for any reason state funding was inadequate or the enrollment dropped, enough time remained to cancel the search.

The improvement in this hiring system was the direct result of the action team's efforts.

Equipment Category

The action team discovered an abundance of information when the **Equipment Category** was dissected. In fact, the thorough evaluation of this category would eventually lead to major root causes and yield the greatest savings.

Having insufficient equipment for the laboratories was one of the reasons the new dean of the School of Arts & Sciences did not schedule additional sections of lab-based science courses. The laboratory equipment was overused, old, and in need of repair. His plea for additional equipment allocation funds went unheeded. Although no matching funds were available, as required by most federal granting agencies, the academic vice president prodded the dean to encourage faculty to write equipment grants. However, the faculty were so busy with teaching overloads that they had little time for grant writing.

However, what appeared to be a snide comment from an unknown source led to a major breakthrough. The comment: "Under Subscribed Programs Have Too Much of the Equipment $."

To compare program efficiency with equipment resource allocation, the action team members obtained data from the Office of Institutional Research & Planning on class enrollments, number of majors per program, cost per major, and cost per credit hour. They dissected the course offerings over the past five years by semester. They worked with each department chair to determine the optimal class sizes for every course. They were determined to practice "management by fact." They gathered these data for each department and placed the data in a spreadsheet format, as shown below.

Course # & Title	# Credits	# Load Hours	# of Sections During the Fall & Spring Semesters								Average # Sections/Yr	Class Sizes			
			91F	91S	92F	92S	93F	93S	94F	94S		Min	Max	Avg	Recomm.

Since a full teaching load translated into 24 load hours per year, the action team was able to determine how many faculty were required to teach each course. For example, if a particular lab course consisted of six load hours, and if four sections were offered every academic year, 1.0 FTE faculty would be required to teach that particular course. Therefore, the action team could determine the theoretical number of faculty each department needed to deliver instruction. Much to its chagrin, the team discovered that many departments recommended class sizes of 35 in the major — but only nine to 15 students enrolled in many of the classes. In spite of the low enrollments, it was common to schedule multiple sections of these upper-division courses each semester, rather than offer fewer sections in order to encourage increased class size and raise productivity.

Furthermore, there were a number of courses that could have been offered either every other year or every third year, as they not only had low enrollments but were offered either as enrichment courses for the "better" students or as ego enhancements for professors who wanted to teach in their specialization. Certain courses were offered through habit and could have been eliminated, as they were not necessary for either the major or for support purposes.

The action team reported that the university was carrying three separate programs for which there was little or no demand. Since all of these programs required the equivalent of only two FTE faculty in an institution with over 400 FTE faculty, and since these faculty were in a technology program that did not teach general education courses, they were ignored or overlooked. These three technology-based programs were not only under-subscribed, but they also commanded a large share of the equipment budget. If these resources were reallocated to cover for the laboratory-based, general education science courses, additional seats could have been added to all of the sections.

Further examination of these data also revealed that certain upper-division courses in the sciences had low enrollments. This was suggested in a posted comment under the **Procedures Category** (see Figure 3.2). Likewise, it was discovered that many of the upper-division courses were unnecessary for the major and could have been offered less frequently with no adverse effect on students.

Additionally, the action team discovered that introductory statistics courses were offered in six of the 21 academic departments; that basic research courses were offered in four departments; and that beginning computer science courses were offered in five departments. In several instances, the same books were used! Furthermore, the enrollments in many of these courses were never at a maximum because of departmental competition.

The action team made far-reaching recommendations, many of which were implemented immediately by the academic departments. The university was able to recoup the equivalent of 15 FTE faculty by phasing out the under-subscribed programs and retraining the retrenched faculty, and by better scheduling courses. This meant that a sufficient number of general education courses could be offered, and that class sizes could be reduced significantly without hiring additional faculty. (Interestingly enough, however, the action team's recommendation of concentrating the statistics courses in the Mathematics Department, the research courses in the Psychology Department, and the computer science courses in the Computer Science Department did not come to fruition.)

In order for equipment repairs to be done in a timely manner, the action team recommended the hiring of a service technician for the Division of Science & Technologies in place of a new faculty member. This was done.

The action team also recommended that the academic vice president set aside at least 2% of the equipment allocation money for matching funds for equipment grants. This was done. As a result, the faculty began to write equipment grants.

Materials Category

Since additional courses were scheduled the day before classes were to begin, the faculty would seldom have sufficient supplies and materials for the lab-based courses. When the action team diagrammed the budgeting system on a flow chart, the chart demonstrated that budgeting was operated as a "blue sky" procedure. Furthermore, the budgeting system was unrelated to the actual need or to the approved goals in the master plan — it had become known as the "black hole" approach. In essence, the department chair, in consultation with the faculty, submitted a budget request with detailed justifications. The dean, after consulting with the department chair, submitted the school's budget request with additional justifications. The academic vice president took the requests and met with the Council of Vice Presidents — these meetings were labeled the "black hole," since very little feedback was received until the actual budgets were allocated. Several months later the vice presidents made a final recommendation to the president, who either approved or modified the budget.

The results of this approach were negative because the high expectations of the unit heads failed to materialize and, over time, the faculty, chairs, and deans became demoralized and found the entire process to be a bureaucratic joke. The action team suggested that the Council of Vice Presidents and the president consider developing a formula-driven budget that would drive the action objectives in the master plan. A separate action team was appointed by the president to examine the benefits of implementing such a revised system. Considerations for developing a formula-driven budget are discussed in the Appendix I.

The **Materials Category** is a good example of how poor management prevents the professors from doing a quality job and how the lack of support by management eventually manifests itself as poor quality in the classroom.

Procedures Category

As mentioned above under the **Equipment Category** section, the inefficiency of scheduling courses, including upper-division courses for majors, was addressed effectively. To increase the numbers of upper-division majors, especially in the sciences, action team members recommended a two-pronged approach. First, they suggested that programs with few majors develop "2+2" articulation agreements with community colleges in order to encourage potential students to transfer to the university after successfully completing their associate degrees. Second, the action team, after confirming the high "failure" rate in the science courses by freshmen and sophomores (in spite of the high use of tutoring services by these students), suggested that a peer-mentoring system be established.

During the next several years, over 100 program-specific "2+2" articulation agreements were established between the science programs and various programs at community colleges. Recently, several of the science departments have established "clubs" on the campuses of community colleges. One unanticipated benefit is that these clubs have caused a significant number of minority students to transfer to the university.

Before the School of Arts & Sciences began a peer-mentoring program, the dean formed a special committee to study the project. As a result, several committee members attended a national conference on mentoring. They reported that the retention rate of students was apparently influenced greatly by class attendance and where students sat in class. They reported that a university in California increased the retention rate from the freshman to the sophomore years by 30% by simply calling the students who missed class and asking why they did not attend; they also found that high-risk students who sat in the first row, the middle two-thirds of the second row, or the middle one-third of the third row had a much better chance of being retained than those who sat in the back rows.

With this basic knowledge, the committee recommended to the dean and to the action team that:

- A student mentoring system be established out of the office of the dean.
- The students who were to do the mentoring (the "Ambassadors") be given proper training on interview techniques.
- A survey instrument be developed in conjunction with the Psychology Department to measure the effectiveness of the mentoring.
- All professors report to the Office of the Dean (via the department chair) any student who missed class.

After the second absence, the Ambassadors were to phone or contact the students directly and ask why they were absent from class. The students were to be informed that the **dean** was concerned about their attendance, since their success was greatly diminished if they did not attend class. The data were to be collected and the results entered on the survey form. (It should be noted that faculty from the School of Arts & Sciences voted to support this mentoring project, and it was conducted as proposed.)

If the student missed a third class, he or she was contacted by a staff member from the Office of the Dean. An appointment was made between the student (customer) and the dean (provider) to discuss the reasons why the student was cutting class.

At this point, the root causes of many potential non-persisters were identified. It was discovered that many of the potential non-persisters could be helped by giving them personal student mentors, many of whom were of similar ethnic backgrounds. In other cases, it was important that the mentor simply be "smart" in the subject in which the student was having difficulty.

For those students who failed to keep their appointments, another surprise awaited them. The dean personally made a visit to a class in which the student was registered. He told the student that he expected him or her to be in his office by the end of the day to talk about class attendance.

The project expanded to include many different types of mentors. For example, almost every faculty member and staff member at the school became a mentor to a student. The students who were on suspension, and who later were granted re-admission, were expected to sit in the first row of every class and act as mentors to those students who were on the verge of failing out and/or not attending class. If they did not agree to this condition, the dean simply denied them re-admission.

Later, the upper-division students acted as mentors to the lower-division students. And successful freshmen and sophomore students formed mentoring groups for grades 6-12 in the regional schools.

Not only did the faculty form clubs at the local community colleges — in which they acted as mentors — but many of the successful juniors and seniors accompanied them to the club meetings and gave advice on "how to beat the system," i.e., how to better their chances of getting through college.

As the mentoring project matured, the school considered the "student failure rate" as an "institutional failure." Increasingly, everyone began to ask, "Where did we fail?" Students were considered customers, and "the customer is always right" attitude began to guide the system. With the "2+2" articulation agreements, the community college clubs, and the dramatically increasing student retention rates, the upper-division enrollments improved to such a degree that the main problem appeared to be the need for additional upper-division courses to meet the needs of majors!

The student-retention project spawned another suggestion from the mentoring committee — that the school consider using several **Learning Community Concepts**, since it appeared these methods dramatically increased the retention of students as well as students' ability to retain content. This recommendation is being implemented by a cross-functional action team of faculty, administrators, and scheduling personnel. Results are expected to be reported soon.

At the end of 18 months, the action team had finally concluded its study on the Recruiting & Admissions office system, the Institutional Research & Planning system, the School Deans system, and the Department Chair system in the production of course schedules (see Figure 3.1). Now the schools were submitting accurate and reasonable schedules in a timely manner to the academic dean. But since the scheduling problems still persisted, the action team examined the Academic Dean system as well.

The action team discovered, even after the school deans submitted error-free schedules in a timely manner, that up to eight months passed between the initial request for the dean to submit class schedules and the actual publication of the final schedule. To exacerbate matters, the final schedule contained many errors. Obviously, it wasn't done right the first time.

The action team created a flow chart of the processes in the Academic Dean system. Figure 3.6 shows the various tasks that were performed in order to produce a class schedule. These tasks are described below.

1.   The academic dean wrote a memo to the associate dean of academic affairs requesting that she begin the process of producing a schedule. (In order not to belabor the point, we will mention the following involvement of personnel only once: the secretary had to type the

memo, the academic dean had to sign the memo, the secretary had to mail it to the associate dean of academic affairs, and the mail room personnel had to deliver the mail. When the mail arrived at the Office of the Associate Dean of Academic Affairs, the secretary had to open and sort the mail and bring the item to the associate dean's attention. (The same would be true for the offices of the 21 chairs and three school deans.)

2.   The associate dean for academic affairs wrote a memo to the 21 department chairs with copies to the three school deans asking the chairs to complete a gridsheet. The gridsheet took the form of a spreadsheet. It had the following entries:

- Department name
- Course section
- Course number
- Course title
- Days scheduled
- Time scheduled
- Credit Hours (CH) of the course
- Professor's name

The gridsheet had several major drawbacks. First, it had to be completed by hand. A typed or computer-generated sheet was unacceptable. Second, credit hours (CH) differed from faculty load hours (LH). The faculty were paid by load hours, and one could not receive the necessary information from the gridsheets about the projected faculty workload. Only CH's were entered, and LH's did not necessarily correlate with CH's, especially in the case of lab courses or courses that had combined lecture sections but different clinical, lab, or discussion sections. The data entry problem was the result of poor computer programming from a unit not directly responsible for the preparation of courses — or so they thought. One of the major causes of the scheduling fiasco was poor leadership in the department of computer services, a major supplier of the process.

3.   The department chairs submitted their recommended schedules to their school dean.

4.   The school deans, after consultation with the chairs, submitted the revised gridsheets (course schedules) to the academic dean.

5.   The academic dean forwarded the proposed schedules to the associate academic dean.

6.   The associate academic dean assigned a clerk to enter each and every course from the gridsheets into the computer main frame. (As mentioned above, the computer program

could not differentiate between courses that had shared lecture sections and separate lab sections. As a result, the data indicated that some faculty were greatly overloaded while others were teaching at a significant underload. In spite of these observations, the members of the department of computer services denied that they were part of the problem!)

Figure 3.6

Flow chart of the course scheduling system

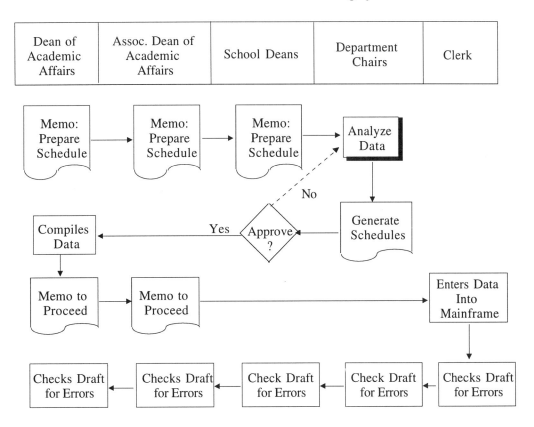

7.   The finalized schedule, including all the errors entered by the chairs, the department sec-retaries, the dean, and the clerk in the Office of the Associate Dean of Academic Affairs, as well as the errors in the computer program, required at least **three** additional cycles of the first eight steps in order to produce a schedule that required no more than **six** errata sheets after being published!

After the action team looked into the problem, it recommended an obvious solution: utilize the campus' electronic mail technology — a process that empowered the chairpersons and the dean — to enter error-free schedules directly onto the main frame via electronic mail. What previously had taken eight months to accomplish now took five working days! The recommended process is shown in Figure 3.7.

This case study demonstrates how TQI philosophy tools can greatly improve the efficiency of institutions of higher education.

Figure 3.7

Revised schema for the scheduling of courses

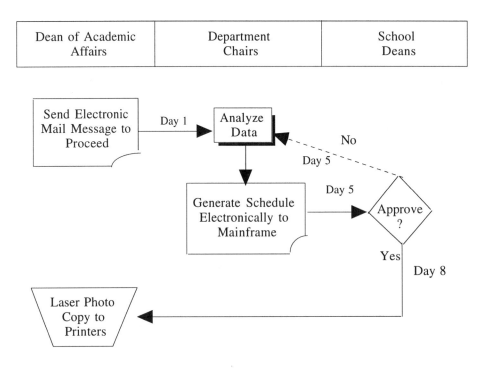

CHAPTER 4: IMPLEMENTING THE SUGGESTIONS

Implementing the suggestions from an action team can be one of the most difficult things to do — it requires trust. Only administration can give trust, as it controls 85-95% of the systems. When trust is accepted, pride in professional work will result in quality. The successful implementation of the recommendations will breed additional trust. Trust breeds pride. Pride breeds quality. And a continuous increase in quality breeds a quality culture. With a quality culture comes organizational stability as the institution attracts more of the market share of potential students — if not more of the market, at least that portion of the market that is better ("better," of course, is defined in terms of their attraction to a quality school).

After the action team makes its recommendations to administration, the president or appropriate vice president should implement the recommendations, form an implementation action team, or do both.

The implementation action team should consist of at least three or four members from the recommending action team and three or four managers who have decision-making responsibilities and who will be affected by the recommendations. The charge: find ways to implement as many of the suggestions as possible as soon as possible.

In order to accomplish this difficult charge, the implementation action team could have used the **Scenario Builder** tool, the **Force Field Analysis** tool, and/or a **Systematic Diagram** to help determine the necessary actions to implement the suggested changes and the probable outcomes of implementing the recommendations. In this case, the team chose the **Scenario Builder**.

The implementation team examined the action team's substantial evidence that the School of Arts & Sciences had costly, under-subscribed programs and also scheduled classes inefficiently. The action team had recommended first that the under-subscribed programs be eliminated and that the two faculty be retrained to teach courses that serve the general education needs of the university.

Second, it recommended that the courses for either majors and/or general education that did not have full classes be scheduled less frequently, in order to assure maximum productivity.

Finally, it recommended that the curricula be modified to reflect more the current needs of the students and less of the needs of faculty. Although it would have been best to examine the recommendations separately when using the Scenario Builder, this group looked broadly into implementing the changes as an entire package. The result is described on the following pages.

Scenario Builder Results if Recommendations are Implemented in the School of Arts & Sciences

C (Changes): (1) the under-subscribed programs should be eliminated and the two faculty retrained to teach general education courses, (2) the courses for either the majors or for general education that routinely do not have full classes should be scheduled less frequently in order to increase productivity, and (3) the curricula should be modified to reflect the present needs of the student body rather than the needs of the faculty (i.e., fewer upper-division electives should be offered).

Scenario 1

1.0   The equipment money usually allocated to the programs that would be eliminated could be reallocated (+10).

1.1   Additional equipment could be assigned to equipment-intensive general education courses (+7).
- Additional workstations could be provided (+10).
- Quality of education could be increased (+10).
- Sizes of laboratory courses could be increased (-10).

1.2   Modern equipment could be purchased (+3).

1.3   Equipment reallocation funds could be directed into upper-division courses for the majors (+8).
- Science majors would be better educated (+7).
- A better reputation could develop for the major, and enrollments would increase (+2).
- This would cause hard feelings among various science faculty (-10).

1.4   Management would reallocate the equipment money to other divisions in the university (-10).
- The president would use the money for his pet projects (-10).
- The academic vice president would reallocate money into the School of Education, as he does not understand the needs of the hard sciences (-50).
- The university as a whole would benefit because all programs need the support. (+10).

Scenario 2

2.0 Better scheduling would increase the class sizes for the courses in the majors, and productivity would increase (+50).

2.1 The science majors would not have as wide a variety of experiences as those in similar institutions, and this would decrease their chances for being accepted into graduate school (-5).

2.2 The increase in class sizes would reduce assessment and the quality of instruction (-8).
* Essay and critical thinking questions would be reduced considerably from routine testing (-7).
* Individualized instruction would be reduced considerably (-10).
* The science faculty would revolt against the increase in class sizes (-10).

2.3 We would be recognized as a leader in productivity in the state system (+6).

2.4 We would have a better handle on the supplies and equipment that would be required for the classes, as we would be better able to predict the class schedules (+8).
* We would be able to order many supplies in bulk and save money (+50).
* The equipment would wear out quicker with the increase in class sizes   (-7).
* We could update the lab experiments more frequently (+10).

Scenario 3

3.0 The curricula for the majors would be updated and would reflect the needs of the "customers" (+50).

3.1 The School of A&S and the departments could form meaningful community advisory councils (+50).
* The curricula could reflect the needs of major employers (+50).
* The graduates would be in greater demand (+10).
* The community advisory council and the graduates would become strong advocates for the school and their majors, and this would help us with future PR and funding (+50).

3.2 The School of A&S and each department would have a "Constancy of Purpose" — Deming's first point (+10).
* Continuous improvement of the curriculum would become routine (+50).
* Long-range planning would become meaningful (+10).
* Innovation and research would suffer (-10).

3.3 The university would become nothing but a vocational school (-10).
- Many faculty would leave (-10).
- The administration, faculty, and governing board would not permit this to happen (+10).
- We would have to recruit vigorously for liberal arts majors (+10).

3.4 The faculty would need constant updating to stay abreast of the scientific and social needs of the students (+10).
- Additional support for travel and professional development would be necessary (+10).
- Additional travel and professional development funds would not be allocated, and the faculty would be expected to use their own money to stay current (-6).
- Some faculty may have to work part-time in industry in order to remain current with the latest equipment and technologies (+6).

Scenario 4

4.0 The School of A&S could have two additional full-time, tenure-track faculty to teach general education courses (+10).

4.1 The additional faculty could reduce the strain on the present faculty, who are trying to meet the needs for general education and for the major (+10).
- The class sizes of the general education courses could be reduced (+8).
- Reduced overloads for the present faculty could result in grant writing, community and university service, and research (+7).
- Management would admit more students, and we would soon revert to the previous crisis situation (-8).

4.2 The new faculty would greatly improve the advising of students (+5).

4.3 The new faculty would leave if they taught only general education courses (-10).
- The new faculty would become incorporated into a department curriculum, and they would teach fewer general education (-10).
- Each department would have to examine how it offers its courses and would be required to schedule courses on an equitable basis (+10).
- Teamwork would keep the new faculty (+5).

4.4 The new faculty would increase the service we offer through continuing education as well as through the committees (+5).

Scenario 5

5.0   The retrenched faculty would leave (-7).

5.1   We would have to seek approval for two new positions (-50).
- This would result in major improvements in the "hiring" system (+2).
- The academic vice president would reallocate these positions to the College of Education, as she does not understand the needs of the hard sciences (-5).
- The money spent on advertising and recruiting would come out of funds that could be used for additional supplies and equipment (-10).

5.2   This would result in additional overloads for faculty (-10).
- This would result in additional stress and poor morale (-10).
- An increase in pay would be welcomed (+5).
- Poor faculty evaluations would result, since they would not have time to do research and service as required by promotion criteria (-10).

5.3   All seven science departments would "fight" for the two positions resulting from the departures from Technology (-50).
- This would result in additional stress and poor morale (-10).
- No one would want to serve on the selection committee (-7).
- The positions would help reduce the overloads and class sizes once the faculty are on board, regardless of the department (+10).

5.4   New faculty would bring new ideas (+5).

Scenario 6

6.0   Many senior faculty who routinely teach specialized courses at the junior and senior levels would leave (-50).

6.1   This would result in additional overloads for faculty (-10).
- This would result in additional stress and poor morale (-10).
- An increase in pay would be welcomed (+5).
- Poor faculty evaluations would result, since they would not have time to do research and service as required by the promotions criteria (-7).

6.2   All seven science departments would "fight" for the available positions (-50).
- This would result in additional stress and poor morale (-10).
- No one would want to serve on the selection committee (-7).
- The positions would help reduce the overloads and class sizes once the faculty are on board, regardless of the department. (+5).

6.3 The science departments would be better able to readjust the curricula to the modern
     world as newly graduated faculty with modern ideas could be hired (+10).
     - This would result in additional stress and poor morale (-10).
     - Younger faculty could be hired on a lower pay scale and, therefore, a greater
       number could be employed. As a result, the additional sections of courses and
       the class size issue could be solved (+10).
     - Innovation and research would increase (+4).

6.4 The university would receive poor PR in the regional papers (-8).
     - This would result in additional stress and poor morale (-10).
     - The public would support the move since they believe that the professoriate
       does not really earn their keep (-10).
     - The president would become more sensitive to the needs of the sciences, and he
       would not permit radical action that would harm the reputation of the university
       (+10).

Using the scoring as described in the procedure for the **Scenario Builder** tool in Section II,
the implementation team obtained the results as shown in Figure 4.1 on the next page.

Figure 4.1
Scenario Builder tally sheet for estimating perceived effects
of change in a process or a system, and the prospect that a given event will occur

1. +10
1.1 +7	1.2 +3	1.3 +8	1.4 -10
1.1.1 +10	1.2.1 ____	1.3.1 +7	1.4.1 - 10
1.1.2 +10	1.2.2 ____	1.3.2 +2	1.4.2 - 50
1.1.3 - 10	1.2.3 ____	1.3.3 -10	1.4.3 +10
Total +27	Total ____	Total +7	Total - 60

2. +50
2.1 - 5	2.2 - 8	2.3 +6	2.4 +8
2.1.1 ____	2.2.1 - 7	2.3.1 ____	2.4.1 +50
2.1.2 ____	2.2.2 - 10	2.3.2 ____	2.4.2 - 7
2.1.3 ____	2.2.3 - 10	2.3.3 ____	2.4.3 +10
Total ____	Total - 35	Total ____	Total +61

3. +50
3.1 +50	3.2 +10	3.3 - 10	3.4 +10
3.1.1 +50	3.2.1 +50	3.3.1 - 10	3.4.1 +10
3.1.2 +10	3.2.2 +10	3.3.2 +10	3.4.2 - 6
3.1.3 +50	3.2.3 - 10	3.3.3 +10	3.4.3 +6
Total +160	Total +60	Total 0	Total +20

4. +10
4.1 +10	4.2 +5	4.3 - 10	4.4 +5
4.1.1 +8	4.2.1 ____	4.3.1 - 10	4.4.1 ____
4.1.2 +7	4.2.2 ____	4.3.2 +10	4.4.2 ____
4.1.3 - 8	4.2.3 ____	4.3.3 +10	4.4.3 ____
Total +17	Total ____	Total 0	Total ____

5. - 7
5.1 - 50	5.2 - 10	5.3 - 50	5.4 +5
5.1.1 +2	5.2.1 - 10	5.3.1 - 10	5.4.1 ____
5.1.2 - 5	5.2.2 +5	5.3.2 - 7	5.4.2 ____
5.1.3 -10	5.2.3 - 10	5.3.3 +10	5.4.3 ____
Total -70	Total - 25	Total - 57	Total ____

6. - 50
6.1 - 10	6.2 - 50	6.3 +10	6.4 - 8
6.1.1 - 10	6.2.1 - 10	6.3.1 - 10	6.4.1 - 10
6.1.2 +5	6.2.2 - 7	6.3.2 +10	6.4.2 - 10
6.1.3 - 7	6.2.3 +5	6.3.3 +4	6.4.3 +10
Total - 22	Total - 62	Total +14	Total -18

Here's how the action team interpreted results from the aforementioned Scenario Builder (for an explanation of the methodology, see Section II).

Step 1: Spell out the recommended changes

In order to increase efficiency, the action team recommended that the School of Arts & Sciences do the following:

- Eliminate the under-subscribed programs and have the two affected faculty retrained to teach general education courses.
- Schedule less frequently the courses (for either the majors or for general education) that routinely have classes that are not full.
- Modify the curricula to reflect the needs of the student body more than the needs of the faculty (e.g., offer fewer upper-division electives).

Step 2: Examine the scores of the six first-level scenarios

All first-level scenarios should have 70% or greater perceived probability of occurring if the changes were implemented. In this case, all six do.

Step 3: Build upon the second-level scenarios that have a 70% or greater perceived probability of occurring

Examining Figure 4.1, the team had to address scenarios 1.1, 1.3, 1.4, 2.2, 2.4, 3.1, 3.2, 3.3, 3.4, 4.1, 4.3, 5.2, 5.3, 6.1, 6.2, 6.3, and 6.4.

Step 4: Describe what will likely happen to each event and what ACTION STEP needs to be taken to accentuate positive and minimize negative outcomes

Scenario 1

The equipment money usually allocated to programs that would be eliminated could be reallocated (+10). Additional equipment could be purchased and assigned to equipment-intensive general education courses (+7). As a result, additional workstations could be provided for the laboratories (+10), and the quality of the educational experience could be increased. However, management would probably increase the class size of the laboratories (-10).

A real threat is that the department chairs would use the additional equipment money for the upper-division courses, which are primarily for the majors (+8). Although a real case could be made that the money is required to better educate the science majors (+7), and those science faculty who teach the introductory courses would have hard feelings (-10).

If additional equipment money became available from the action taken by faculty in the School of Arts & Sciences, management would reallocate most of it to another division of the university (-10). If the president didn't use the money to remodel his house (-10), the vice president for academic affairs would reallocate a large portion to the School of Education, as he does not understand the needs of the hard sciences (-50). But the university as a whole would benefit from the support given any program, as all programs need support (+10).

ACTION STEP: The dean must get a firm commitment from the president and the vice president of academic affairs that if the faculty in the School of Arts & Sciences were to make sacrifices resulting in substantial savings, the money would be reallocated into the science equipment fund for the next five years.

DESIRED OUTCOME: The faculty and management would develop trust and work together as a team for the good of the students.

Scenario 2

Better scheduling would increase the class sizes for the courses in the majors, and productivity would increase (+50). However, the faculty would argue that the increase in class sizes in the upper-division major courses would reduce assessment and the quality of instruction (-8). As a result:

1. Essay and critical thinking questions would be reduced considerably from the routine testing (-7).
2. Individualized instruction would be reduced considerably (-10).
3. The science faculty would revolt against the increase in class sizes (-10).

We would also have a better handle on the supplies and equipment that would be required for the classes, as we would be better able to predict the class schedules (+8). Thus:

1. We would be able to order many supplies in bulk and save money (+50).
2. The equipment would wear out quicker with the increase in class sizes (-7).
3. We could update the laboratory experiments more frequently (+10).

ACTION STEP: A task force consisting mainly of the science faculty should be established by the dean to reaffirm the recommended class sizes for the service courses and for the courses in each major. The task force should report its recommendations back to the school.

DESIRED OUTCOME: The faculty in the School of A&S would realize that better scheduling of the upper-division courses for the majors and elimination of the under-subscribed programs would actually reduce the class sizes of the general education courses, which consist largely of freshmen who need more individualized instruction in order to succeed. They would also realize the benefits of "bulk" buying power and updated laboratory experiments.

Scenario 3

The curricula for the majors would be updated and would reflect the needs of the "customers" (+50). This would permit the dean and each of the academic departments to form community advisory councils (+50). Thus:

1.   The curricula could reflect the needs of the major employers of our graduates (+50).
2.   Our graduates would be in greater demand (+10).
3.   The community advisory council and the graduates would become strong advocates for the school and their majors. This would help us with future PR and funding (+50).

The focused curricula would permit the School of A&S and each department to have a clear mission (+10). As a result:

1.   Continuous improvement of the curriculum will become routine (+50).
2.   Long-range planning would become meaningful (+10).
3.   Innovation and research would suffer (-10). (It should be noted that this prediction was wrong. In fact, after the action team gathered additional data, the opposite was found to be true.)

The up-to-date, focused curricula would require constant training of the faculty in order to keep them breast of the scientific needs of the students (+10). This means:

1.   Additional support for travel and professional development would be necessary (+10).
2.   Additional travel and professional development funds might not be allocated, and the faculty would be expected to use their own money to stay current (-6).
3.   Some faculty may have to work part-time in industry in order to remain current with the latest equipment and technologies (+6).

ACTION STEP: The dean should address the benefits to the faculty of Scenario 3.
DESIRED OUTCOME: Faculty support.

Scenario 4

The School of Arts & Sciences could have two additional full-time, tenure-track faculty to teach general education courses (+10). The additional faculty could reduce the strain on the present faculty, who are trying to meet not only the needs for general education, but also the needs for the major (+10). This could result in a reduction of the class sizes in the general education courses (+8), as well as reduced overloads for the present faculty, which could result in grant writing, community and university service, and research (+7). By the same token, management could admit additional students, and we would soon revert to the previous crisis situation (-8). The new faculty hired to teach only the general education courses would soon leave (-10).

ACTION STEP: The dean should approach the vice president for academic affairs in order to get a meaningful budgeting process that takes into account class sizes, the equipment intensity of courses, and the level of courses.

DESIRED OUTCOME: Perhaps a formula-driven budget could be developed, or some other budgeting process that would not penalize general education, laboratory-based courses and the faculty who teach them.

Scenario 5

The retrenched faculty would leave (-7) and we would have to seek approval for two new positions through the bureaucratic hiring process (-50). The money spent on advertising and recruiting would come out of the funds that could be used for additional supplies and equipment (-10), which might result in additional overloads for faculty (-10). This would result in additional stress and poor morale (-10), as well as poor faculty evaluations, since faculty would not have time to do research and service as required by the promotions criteria (-10). In addition, all seven science departments would compete for the two positions (-50). Therefore:

1.   This would result in additional stress and poor morale (-10).
2.   No one would want to serve on the selection committee (-7).
3.   The positions would help reduce the overloads and class sizes once the faculty are on board, regardless of the department (+10).

ACTION STEP: The dean should approach the vice president for academic affairs in order to get a meaningful budgeting process that takes into account class sizes, the equipment intensity of courses, and the level of courses. A completely revised hiring approval system needs to be developed as well, and the dean must bring this to the attention of the vice presidents.

DESIRED OUTCOME: Perhaps a formula-driven budget could be developed, or some other budgeting process that would not penalize general education laboratory-based courses and the faculty who teach them. In addition, the present faculty hiring system must be re-examined so that faculty can be hired in a timely fashion.

Scenario 6

Many senior faculty who routinely teach specialized courses at the junior and senior levels would leave (-50). This would result in additional overloads for the remaining faculty (-10). Thus:

1. Additional stress and lowering of morale would result (-10).
2. An increase in pay due to the overloads would be welcomed (+5).
3. Poor faculty evaluations would result, since faculty would not have time to do research and service (as required by the promotions criteria) because they will be teaching (-7).

All seven science departments would "fight" for the available positions (-50). As a result:

1. Additional stress and lowering of morale would result (-10).
2. No one would want to serve on the selection committee (-7).
3. The positions would help reduce the overloads and class sizes once the new faculty are hired, regardless of the department (+5).

The science departments would be better able to readjust the curricula to the modern world, as newly graduated faculty with updated knowledge could be hired (+10). As a result:

1. Additional stress and lowering of morale will result (-10).
2. Younger faculty could be hired at a lesser pay scale, so a greater number could be employed. As a result, the issues revolving around the last-minute addition of courses/sections and the increasing of class sizes could be solved (+10).
3. Innovation and research will increase (+4). (It should be noted that the action team found this was incorrect after doing a search of the literature.)

The university will receive poor press if many of the senior faculty leave (-8). As a result:

1. Additional stress and lowering of morale would result (-10).
2. The public would support the move, since they believed the professoriate does not really earn their keep (-10).
3. The president would become more sensitive to the needs of the sciences, and he would not permit radical action that would harm the reputation of the university (+10).

ACTION STEP: The dean should appoint a task force consisting mainly of senior faculty from the sciences to address the issue of senior faculty turnover and the benefits and drawbacks of reducing the number and frequency of specialized courses. The task force should be instructed to use Force Field Analysis, Relations Diagramming, and Systematic Diagramming in analyzing its recommendations. The task force should report back to the school within two months.

DESIRED OUTCOME: Faculty understanding and support toward an orderly transition of change, with many of the senior faculty supporting the need for change rather than leaving the university.

Step 5: List and analyze any scenario that has a total whose absolute value exceeds 100 (greater than +100/less than -100)

The scenarios that have an absolute value exceeding 100 are scenarios 2.4, 3.1, 3.2, and 6.2. Scenarios receiving a high score usually indicate that if the recommended changes are implemented, and if the action team's perceptions are representative of the actual institutional culture, these events would probably be the outcome.

Scenario 2.4: We would have a better handle on supplies and equipment that would be required for the classes, as we would be better able to predict the class schedules (+8).

- We would be able to order many supplies in bulk and save money (+50).
- The equipment would wear out quicker with the increase in class sizes (-7).
- We could update the laboratory experiments more frequently (+10).

Scenario 3.1: The School of A&S and the departments could form meaningful community advisory councils (+50).

- The curricula could reflect the needs of the major employers of our graduates (+50).
- The graduates would be in greater demand (+10).
- The community advisory council and the graduates would become strong advocates for the school and their majors, and this would help us with future PR and funding (+50).

Scenario 3.2: The School of A&S and each department would have a "Constancy of Purpose" — Deming's first point (+10).

- Continuous improvement of the curriculum would become routine (+50).
- Long-range planning would become meaningful (+10).
- Innovation and research would suffer (-10).

Scenario 6.2: All seven science departments would compete for the available positions (-50).

- This would result in additional stress and poor morale (-10).
- No one would want to serve on the selection committee (-7).
- The positions would help reduce the overloads and class sizes once faculty are on board, regardless of the department (+5).

Step 6: Suggest one or two systems that should be improved to maximize the positive and minimize the negative

After analyzing the results of the scenario, the action team decided that two dysfunctional systems were at the root of the major problems, namely, the **Resource Allocation** and **Faculty Hiring** systems.

Step 7: Draw a conclusion

The action team concluded that the dean of the School of A&S must bring to the attention of the academic vice president the need for systems review and improvements in budget allocation, faculty allocation, and faculty hiring. It reported that the academic vice president had to understand that he would continue to have major problems providing sufficient sections and seats for the general education courses without improving the aforesaid systems and increasing the "trust factor" between faculty and administration. By the same token, if these systems were corrected and empowerment of faculty increased, a significant increase in efficiency and productivity would result.

Summary

Chapters 1-4 describe the results of a TQI project in an academic unit within a comprehensive public university. A cross-functional action team was appointed by the academic vice president with this charge: to make specific recommendations improving the registration system, as determined by having scheduled the appropriate number of general education courses with reasonable class sizes to meet the demands of all students three months prior to the first day of scheduled classes. The action team drew a **Flow Chart** to better determine who and what was involved in the production of the schedule. The team concluded that the problems began at the school level with the dean and the department chairs, and ended in chaos in the academic dean's office.

By using **Cause and Effect** diagrams, the action team identified the perceived causes for the insufficient number of general education courses scheduled. The causes were placed into four categories: people, equipment, materials, and procedures.

As it was later discovered, the problem did not involve having insufficient faculty to meet the needs, but in the poor scheduling of courses. By flow-charting the personnel planning system, the action team realized the university could never have a timely personnel plan unless the system changed. Suggestions for changing the personnel planning system were implemented, making the system extremely responsive to the needs of the department chairs.

The better scheduling of classes and the phasing out of under-subscribed programs saved the school over $750,000 a year. This money was reinvested in hiring an electronic repair technician who was able to repair enough equipment to make it possible to schedule additional sections of laboratory-based general education science courses. In addition, better scheduling permitted not only additional sections of much-needed courses, but also smaller class sizes.

As a direct result of the investigation of the action team, the School of Arts & Sciences established "2+2" articulation agreements with community colleges and a peer-mentoring system to increase the number of students majoring in the sciences. These processes were so successful that the previously under-subscribed upper-division courses became cost-efficient. In fact, the number of faculty had to be increased to meet the increased enrollments in the majors!

While the action team was examining the systems that impacted upon the scheduling process, it recommended specific changes to the scheduling system and the budgeting system. The changes made to the academic dean's scheduling system had a great outcome: what previously took eight months to accomplish, with numerous errors, now took eight days, with few errors!

The president has formed a separate action team to look into the possibility of using a formula-driven budgeting system for the university, hoping to make the budgeting system less bureaucratic and more encouraging of efficiency and quality.

It should be noted that management can commit destructive organizational errors either by not recognizing the hard work of an action team or by failing to implement the recommendations without reason. In several institutions, when either of these non-responses occurred, the morale plummeted, and faculty and staff reverted to their "business as usual" routines.

SECTION II: The Tools

AFFINITY DIAGRAM

The **Affinity Diagram** was invented by Kawakita Jiro and is used as a planning tool. Unlike the **Scenario Builder**, which roughly quantifies the outcomes resulting from a change in a system, the Affinity Diagram is more of a creative procedure that tries to organize the issues concerning a process or a problem without quantification.

An Affinity Diagram is especially useful in clarifying a problem or issue that is difficult to understand or is in disarray. One benefit of using the Affinity Diagram at the very beginning of a TQI process is that it helps build consensus among task force members studying the problem.

An Affinity Diagram is rarely used alone. However, when used with the **Scenario Builder**, the **Relations Diagram**, or the **Nominal Group Process**, it can help an action team or task force identify the major root causes of a problem or issue. The group can direct its efforts more efficiently.

Procedure

1. State the problem

Under the direction of a team leader, the team members should arrive at a statement of the problem or issue being addressed. This is best done in the form of a question. For example, "What are the obstacles to establishing TQM throughout the institution?"

2. Record the perceptions

Working alone, each person writes his/her comment on adhesive note paper or on an index card after announcing his/her idea to the group. The purpose of announcing the perception is to permit others to piggyback any related ideas. Only a single idea should be entered on each note card. This proceeds until all of the people have exhausted their perceptions. Remember, as in any brainstorming session, there is no verbal exchange between the members. All of the notes are placed on the wall or in the center of a large conference table. Let's assume the following perceptions (on the next page) are generated and posted. Concerning the questions above:

The president would not permit it.

The vice presidents would not support it.

The deans would not support it.

The faculty would think it is another way to increase productivity without increasing the budget.

The staff would agree with the faculty, and they would be suspicious about the intent of TQM.

The union leadership would consider TQM a management tool to make the union powerless.

The president would feel out of control.

The union would not permit full empowerment of the faculty and staff, as people would be working outside of their job descriptions and would not be compensated for their efforts.

There is a total misunderstanding of what TQM and TQI are all about.

The faculty would not want another committee.

The governing board would not support the thrust toward quality; it is too cheap.

It is too expensive to have a quality university.

We have too many people set in their ways to begin to think about new concepts.

3.   Group similar and/or related perceptions

   The members of the group place their notes into related groups. These are said to have an "affinity" for each other. It is important that the members of the task force do this in silence.

The notes can be moved any number of times. It is not uncommon to have 10 related groups, although one may have as few as three.

The grouping that resulted from the aforementioned example is shown below:

Group 1

> The president would not permit it.

> The vice presidents would not support it.

> The deans would not support it.

> The president would feel out of control.

> The governing board would not support the thrust toward quality; it is too cheap.

Group 2

> The faculty would think it is another way to increase productivity without increasing the budget.

> The staff would agree with the faculty, and they would be suspicious about the intent of TQM.

> The faculty would not want another committee.

Group 3

> The union leadership would consider TQM a management tool to make the union powerless.

> The union would not permit full empowerment of the faculty and staff, as people would be working outside of their job descriptions and would not be compensated for their efforts.

Group 4

> There is a total misunderstanding of what
> TQM and TQI are all about.

> It is too expensive to have a quality university.

> We have too many people set in their ways
> to begin to think about new concepts.

4. Assign a name to each group with a header designation

The team leader reads the notes in each group. Members name each group. The leader writes a header for each group. If there is a miscellaneous group, the task force should examine each perception and, if possible, place each note into a group. In our example, the four groups are:

Group 1
Educate the Administration

> The president would not permit it.

> The vice presidents would not support it.

> The deans would not support it.

> The president would feel out of control.

> The governing board would not support the thrust toward quality;
> it is too cheap.

Group 2
Educate the Faculty & Staff

> The faculty would think it is another way to increase productivity
> without increasing the budget.

> The staff would agree with the faculty, and they would be
> suspicious about the intent of TQM.

> The faculty would not want another committee.

Group 3
Educate the Union Executive Committee

The union leadership would consider TQM a management
tool to make the union powerless.

The union would not permit full empowerment of the faculty and
staff, as people would be working outside of their job descriptions
and would not be compensated for their efforts.

Group 4
Develop and Implement Marketing Procedures

There is a total misunderstanding about what TQM and TQI are
all about.

It is too expensive to have a quality university.

We have too many people set in their ways to
begin to think about the new concepts.

5. Draw the Affinity Diagram

The task force members should tape the notes in each group onto a board or a large flip chart. With the header cards at the top, the leader should draw borders around each group (as shown on the next page).

Affinity Diagram
Obstacles to Establishing TQM

Educate Administration

The president would not permit it.	The president would feel out of control.
The vice presidents would not support it.	The governing board would not support the thrust towards quality; the board is cheap.
The deans would not support it.	

Educate Faculty & Staff

The faculty would think it is another way to increase productivity without increasing the budget.	The faculty would not want another committee.
The staff would be suspicious about the intent of TQM.	

Educate the Union Executive Committee Participate

The union would consider TQM a management tool to make the union powerless.

The union would not permit full empowerment of faculty and staff as people would be working outside of their job descriptions and would not be compensated for their efforts.

Develop and Implement Marketing Procedures

There is a total misunderstanding of what TQM and TQI are all about.

It is too expensive to have a quality university.

We have too many people set in their ways to try new concepts.

6. Discuss each group

The task force members should discuss each group and how it relates to the problem. This will result in a better understanding of the issues and processes making up the problem.

In order to arrive at deeper understandings of each root cause, the task force may want to use a **Relations Diagram** for each of the groups. Depending upon the problem or issue, the **Scenario Builder**, **Systematic Diagram**, and **Cause and Effect** diagrams may be of value.

CAUSE AND EFFECT DIAGRAM

The **Cause and Effect Diagram (CED)** was developed by Kaoru Ishikawa. It is also referred to as an Ishikawa Diagram or a Fishbone Diagram, since it looks like a fish skeleton.

The CED is useful for getting input on the root causes of a specific problem. You can often use it with a **Relations Diagram**, an **Affinity Diagram**, or the **Nominal Group Process**.

Procedure

1. State the problem

Identify a specific problem contributing to a non-quality result. Place it on the far right-hand side of an overhead, flip chart, or sheet of butcher paper.

2. Record the perceptions

After you draw the backbone with the identified problem, add the primary causal category boxes (people, equipment, materials and procedures — some also add environment) and draw arrows to the backbone. This is the beginning of the CED. (Some institutions have reusable 3' x 2' boards with the skeleton and primary causal categories painted on permanently.)

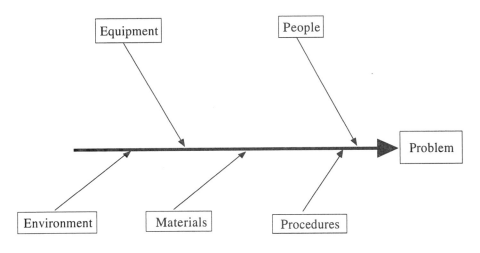

Write the **causes** and **sub-causes** on the adhesive notes and place them in one of the primary causal categories.

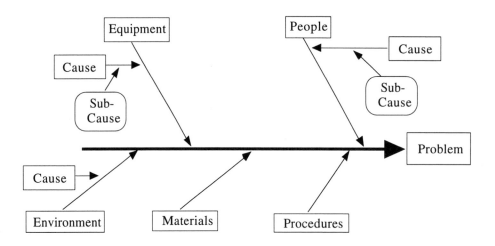

3. Complete the Cause and Effect Diagram

Shown below is the CED outlining the perceptions of faculty as to the causes of poor student evaluations of teaching.

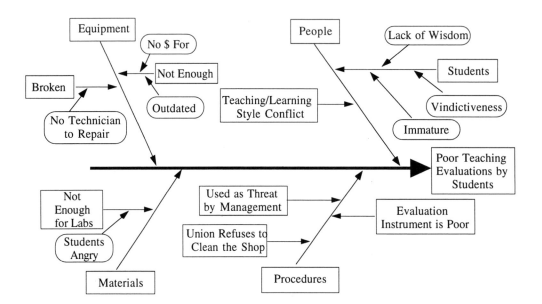

4. Record and discuss the results

This step will help you determine the root causes of the undesired effect or problem. Remember that the purpose of the CED is to generate ideas about the probable causes of the problem and to get everyone involved in submitting suggestions. Therefore, don't tolerate criticism of any idea or comment. Instead, encourage people to build upon the causes and sub-causes posted by others.

5. Other suggestions

If the group identifies a major root cause for a problem, it could become a likely candidate for its own Fishbone analysis.

CONTROL CHARTS

Control Charts are used to test the stability of a system. They measure the number or proportion of non-conforming items. They all have a common centerline that represents a process average and lines that display upper and lower control limits that provide information on the variation. They are used to identify either "common" or "special" causes of variation and to prevent over- or under-control of the processes within a system.

The charts are drawn by gathering samples, called subgroups, from a process, product, or service characteristic. Control limits are based on the variation that occurs within the subgroups. The centerline of the chart is taken to be the estimated mean of the sampling distribution, while the upper control limit (UCL) is the mean plus 3 times the estimated standard error, and the lower control limit (LCL) is the estimated mean minus 3 times the estimated standard error.

We will describe two control charts in detail, namely the **np-chart** and the **p-chart**. Both charts are **attribute** (characteristic) charts in that the characteristic under study gives a yes/no, good/bad, pass/fail, or present/absent answer. The np-chart is used to plot the number of non-conformances when the subgroup size is constant. The p-chart is used to plot the **proportion** of non-conformances when the subgroup size is either **constant** or **variable**.

We'll also give brief descriptions of the **c-chart** and the **u-chart**, which are used when the characteristic under study is too complex for a simple answer.

np-chart

An np-chart is used when the stability of a system is to be measured. The attributes control chart is used when the characteristic under study has a definite yes/no answer, the subgroups are of equal size, the sampling time is consistent, and the data is plotted in the order taken.

Procedure

1. Select the data to be analyzed

We have assumed that the task force or the individual studying a system has collected the attribute data. In the case study below, we'll examine the number of incomplete "work orders" (requests for repair) at the end of the working day for 30 days.

2. Record the data

Record the data in the order in which it was collected. The example on the next page comes from the unit of building and grounds at a state university where the director wanted to know why work orders were not being completed on time.

Data for the np-chart

Day	Sample Size	Number of Incomplete Work Orders	Proportion
1	100	14	0.14
2	100	2	0.02
3	100	11	0.11
4	100	4	0.04
5	100	9	0.09
6	100	7	0.07
7	100	4	0.04
8	100	6	0.06
9	100	3	0.03
10	100	2	0.02
11	100	3	0.03
12	100	8	0.08
13	100	4	0.04
14	100	15	0.15
15	100	5	0.05
16	100	3	0.03
17	100	8	0.08
18	100	4	0.04
19	100	2	0.02
20	100	5	0.05
21	100	5	0.05
22	100	7	0.07
23	100	9	0.09
24	100	1	0.01
25	100	3	0.03
26	100	12	0.12
27	100	9	0.09
28	100	3	0.03
29	100	6	0.06
30	100	9	0.09
Totals	3,000	183	

3. Do the calculations

   You need to calculate the **average**, the **upper control limit** (UCL), and the **lower control limit** (LCL) in order to determine the stability of the system. Note, however, that a minimum of 25 to 30 subgroups is required to calculate the control limits.

3.1   **The average** = total number of incomplete work orders / number of subgroups

$$= \sum np \div 30$$

$$= 14 + 2 + 11 + 4 + ... + 9 \div 30$$

$$= 183 \div 30$$

$$= 6.1$$

This number should be recorded in the space labeled "Avg." in the control chart.

3.2   The **UCL** is calculated using the formula:

$$UCL = \text{Average} + 3 \sqrt{\text{Average} [1 - (\text{Average} \div n)]}$$

$$= 6.1 + 3\sqrt{6.1 [1 - (6.1 \div 100)]}$$

$$= 6.1 + 3\sqrt{6.1 (1 - 0.061)}$$

$$= 6.1 + 3\sqrt{6.1 (0.939)}$$

$$= 6.1 + 3\sqrt{5.728}$$

$$= 6.1 + 3 (2.393)$$

$$= 6.1 + 7.18$$

$$= 13.3$$

This number should be recorded in the space labeled "UCL" in the control chart.

3.3   The **LCL** is calculated using the formula:

$$\text{LCL} = \text{Average} - 3 \sqrt{\text{Average} \left[1 - (\text{Average} \div n) \right]}$$

$$= 6.1 - 3\sqrt{6.1 \left[1 - (6.1 \div 100) \right]}$$

$$= 6.1 - 3\sqrt{6.1 \, (0.939)}$$

$$= 6.1 - 3\sqrt{5.728}$$

$$= 6.1 - 3 \, (2.393)$$

$$= 6.1 - 7.2$$

$$= 0$$

This number should be recorded in the space labeled "LCL" in the control chart. (There can be no negative number.)

4. Draw the chart

First, you need to scale the chart. Begin by determining the largest number in the data and compare this with the UCL number. In our example, the largest number is 15 and the UCL number is 13.3.

A rule of thumb is to count the lines on your chart paper and multiply the amount by 0.66. The chart paper in our example is shown on the next page. It has 30 lines, therefore, 30 x 0.66 = 19.8, or $\approx$ 20.

Starting the np-chart

Product/Service	Chart Type ^ p ^ np ^ c ^ u	Quality Measure		Measurement Device	
Name	Department	Avg =	UCL =	LCL =	Chart No.
Date					
Time					
Discrepancy					
1					
2					
3					
4					
5					
Total					
Proportion					
Sample Size (n)					

Divide the largest number in your example by 20 to obtain your increment value: $15 \div 20 = 0.75$. You will always round the figure upward to the nearest whole number; so in this case, every line will represent 1.

The lines are usually numbered from the bottom up. The bottom line is 0 and every line will represent one incomplete work order. (In other cases, it may be necessary to label the lines with other multiples such as 5, 10, 25, etc.) The attributes control chart, completely labeled according to our example, is shown on the next page.

Labeled np-chart

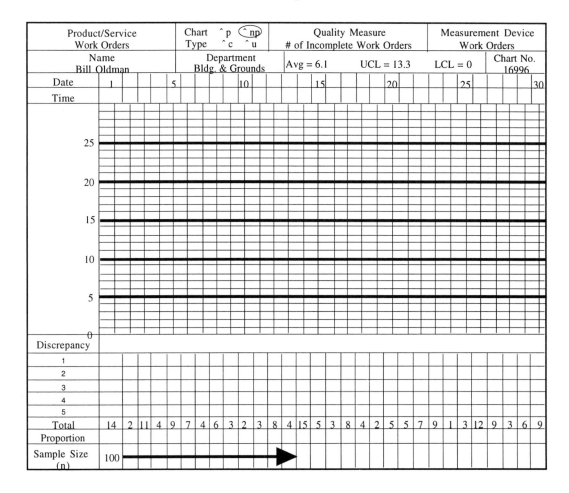

Product/Service Work Orders	Chart Type	^p (np) ^c ^u	Quality Measure # of Incomplete Work Orders		Measurement Device Work Orders	

| Name Bill Oldman | | Department Bldg. & Grounds | Avg = 6.1   UCL = 13.3 | LCL = 0 | Chart No. 16996 |

Now draw the center line (or "average") and the control limits. Then plot the values and connect the points. The completed chart is shown below.

Completed np-chart

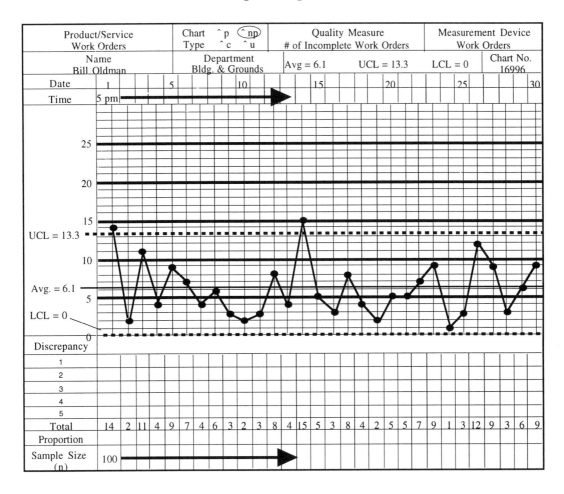

Total	14	2	11	4	9	7	4	6	3	2	3	8	4	15	5	3	8	4	2	5	5	7	9	1	3	12	9	3	6	9

5. Analyze the chart

All control charts are analyzed using basic rules:

- Look for points above or below the control limits.
- Look for a run of seven or more points above or below the average (center line).
- Look for a run of seven or more points either going up or down.
- Look for cyclical patterns.

In our example, the "work order" system appears unstable. On days 1 and 14, the number of incomplete work orders were above the upper control limit, but there is neither a run of seven points above or below the center line nor going up or down; also, there aren't any cyclical patterns.

A note on terms: in this section, we use the term "run" either in the sense of elapsed time or in the sense of direction. If day-plots on the graph stayed above the center line for seven consecutive days, that would constitute a run. Likewise, if for seven consecutive days the day-plots moved consistently in one direction, that would be a run.

The above system appears to have "special causes" as a defect, and improvement in the number of completed work orders could not be undertaken until these special causes were analyzed and addressed and the system was stabilized.

After the director of building and grounds examined what occurred on days 1 and 14, he discovered on each day a new employee came on board — on day 1 a carpenter, on day 14 an electrician. Neither was given proper training in standard operating procedures of how to prioritize work and how to enter data on the forms to demonstrate that the work was completed. The solution was simple: have training sessions for new employees so that they can do the job right the first time!

When first using np-charts you may want to assess the stability of a system and then analyze the factors that contribute to variations. However, after improvements are generated and the system under study is determined to be stable, you may want to collect data in a different way, stratify your data by day of the week, time and location, and redo the np-charts. In the above example, after training sessions and continuing education opportunities for all of the personnel in the department of building and grounds, there may be fewer incomplete work orders in the carpentry unit but no change in the electrical unit. Of course, recalculations of new control limits will eventually be needed, but this should be put off until you have enough data to make the new chart statistically valid.

p-chart

A p-chart is used when you want to plot the proportion of non-conformances and the subgroup size is either constant or variable. Like the np-chart, the p-chart is an attribute control chart that studies a characteristic that has an either/or, pass/fail, yes/no answer. For example:

- A professor may want to plot the proportion of students failing his/her class over the semester.
- A professor may want to plot the proportion of students not completing homework assignments over the semester.

The p-chart, like any control chart, helps determine special and common cause variations in a system, so that proper action can be taken for improvement without exerting over- or under-control. It is used by task forces to help determine the stability of a system and to monitor the improvement of the system after action is taken.

Procedure

1. Select the data to be analyzed

We have assumed that the task force or the individual studying a system has collected the attribute data. In the case study below, we will examine the number of incomplete homework assignments in the course "Introduction to Accounting." The professor had 100 students in his 10 a.m., MWF class, and he gave a homework problem after every class period for 10 of the 15 weeks in the semester. (During the other five weeks, the students had exams and were responsible for discussing the results of a group project.) The homework problem was to be returned the following class period. Several graduate assistants were assigned to collect the homework and return the previous day's homework. Since students drop the class and others leave school, the sample size was variable throughout the semester. (When a student had an excused absence, he or she was permitted to hand in the homework during the first day he or she returned to class.) As a result, the p-chart had to be used.

2. Record the data (as shown on the next page)

Data for the p-chart

k #	Date	n Subgroup Size	np Number of Incomplete Assignments	np ÷ n Proportion
1	9-3	100	15	0.150
2	9-5	100	6	0.060
3	9-7	100	11	0.110
4	9-10	100	4	0.040
5	9-14	94	9	0.096
6	9-17	94	7	0.074
7	9-19	94	4	0.043
8	9-21	94	8	0.085
9	9-24	91	3	0.033
10	9-28	91	2	0.022
11	10-1	91	1	0.011
12	10-3	91	10	0.109
13	10-5	91	7	0.077
14	10-8	91	25	0.275
15	10-12	91	5	0.055
16	10-15	79	3	0.038
17	10-17	79	8	0.101
18	10-19	79	4	0.051
19	10-22	79	2	0.025
20	10-24	79	5	0.063
21	10-26	79	5	0.063
22	10-31	72	7	0.097
23	11-2	72	9	0.125
24	11-5	72	1	0.014
25	11-7	72	3	0.042
26	11-9	72	12	0.167
27	11-12	72	9	0.125
28	11-14	72	3	0.042
29	11-16	72	6	0.083
30	11-19	72	9	0.125
	Totals	2,535	203	0.0801

3. Do the calculations

3.1   The **proportion** for each subgroup has to be calculated. As shown in the previous table, this is accomplished by dividing the total number (np) by the subgroup size (n). In our first entry above, 15 (the number of incomplete homework assignments on September 3) is divided by 100 (sample size). Carry the calculations out to three places.

3.2   The **average proportion** is calculated by taking the total number in the subgroup row (203) and dividing it by the total number in the sample size row (2,535).

$$\text{average proportion } (\overline{p}) = \text{total number} \div \text{number of subgroups}$$
$$= \Sigma np \div n$$
$$= 203 \div 2{,}535$$
$$= 0.0801$$

This number should be recorded in the space labeled "Avg." in the control chart.

3.3   The **average subgroup size** is calculated by dividing the total number of the subgroup size (2,535) by the number of the subgroups taken (k).

$$\text{average subgroup size } (\overline{n}) = \Sigma n \div k$$
$$= 2{,}535 \div 30$$
$$= 84.5$$

3.4   Make certain that the subgroup size doesn't vary more than ± 25% from the average subgroup size (84.5). This is done by multiplying 84.5 by 1.25 for the number greater than 25%, and 84.5 by 0.75 for the number less than 25%.

$$>25\% = 84.5 \text{ x } 1.25 = 105.6$$
$$<25\% = 84.5 \text{ x } 0.75 = 63.4$$

Since none of our sample sizes (n) was higher than 105.6 or less than 63.4, separate calculations for the control limits aren't necessary. If, however, you have subgroup sizes 25% above or below 84.5, you will have to calculate separate UCL's and LCL's on **each** of the points by substituting the appropriate number (n) in the formula shown below. These points with their separate UCL's and LCL's are plotted on the same graph. (Refer to the example in the u-chart at the end of this section.)

3.5   Do the calculations for the control limits

$$\text{UCL} = \bar{p} + 3 \sqrt{\frac{\bar{p}\,(1 - \bar{p})}{\bar{n}}}$$

$$= 0.0801 + 3\sqrt{0.0801\,(1 - 0.0801) \div 84.5}$$

$$= 0.0801 + 3\sqrt{0.0801\,(0.9199) \div 84.5}$$

$$= 0.0801 + 3\sqrt{0.0737 \div 84.5}$$

$$= 0.0801 + 3(0.02953)$$

$$= 0.1687$$

Now calculate the lower control limit:

$$\text{LCL} = \bar{p} - 3 \sqrt{\frac{\bar{p}\,(1 - \bar{p})}{\bar{n}}}$$

$$= 0.0801 - 0.0886$$

$$= 0$$

4. Draw the chart

The scaling and plotting are done in exactly the same manner as in the np-chart. The largest proportion of incomplete homework assignments in our example is 0.275 and 66% of the number of lines in our graph is 20. Therefore, each line has to be $0.275 \div 20 = 0.014$, and since adjusting is always done upward, each line represents 0.020.

The completed chart is shown on the next page.

Completed p-chart

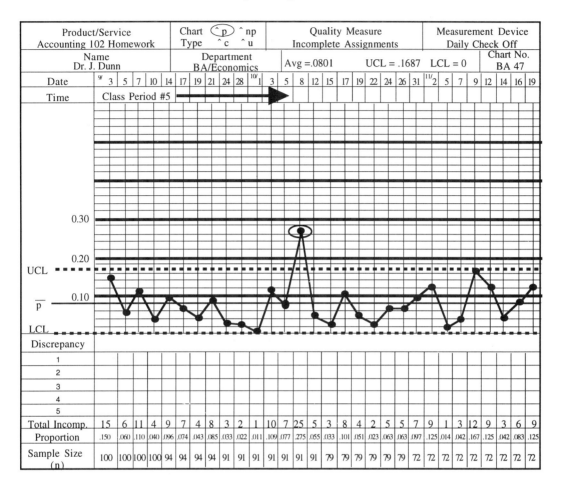

Product/Service	Chart	Type	Quality Measure		Measurement Device		
Accounting 102 Homework	⌢p ^np	^c ^u	Incomplete Assignments		Daily Check Off		

Name		Department				Chart No.
Dr. J. Dunn		BA/Economics	Avg =.0801	UCL = .1687	LCL = 0	BA 47

Analysis points from chart (Date, Total Incomp., Proportion, Sample Size):

Date	9/ 3	5	7	10	14	17	19	21	24	28	10/ 1	3	5	8	12	15	17	19	22	24	26	31	11/ 2	5	7	9	12	14	16	19
Total Incomp.	15	6	11	4	9	7	4	8	3	2	1	10	7	25	5	3	8	4	2	5	5	7	9	1	3	12	9	3	6	9
Proportion	.150	.060	.110	.040	.096	.074	.043	.085	.033	.022	.011	.109	.077	.275	.055	.033	.101	.051	.023	.063	.063	.097	.125	.014	.042	.167	.125	.042	.083	.125
Sample Size (n)	100	100	100	100	94	94	94	94	91	91	91	91	91	91	91	79	79	79	79	79	79	72	72	72	72	72	72	72	72	72

5. Analyze the chart

   All control charts are analyzed using basic rules:

   - Look for points above or below the control limits.
   - Look for a run of seven or more points above or below the average (center line).
   - Look for a run of seven or more points either going up or down.
   - Look for cyclical patterns.

Summary

In our example, the homework system appears to be unstable. On October 8, the number of incomplete homework assignments was above the upper control limit line. However, there is no run of seven points above or below the center line. There is no run of seven points going up or going down, and there are no cyclical patterns.

The above system appears to have "special cause" as a defect, and improvement in the number of completed homework assignments could not be undertaken until these special causes were analyzed and addressed, and the system was stabilized.

After the professor examined what had occurred on October 8, he discovered the cause was the Monday class immediately after the festivities of homecoming weekend. Once this special cause was removed, the system could be considered stable. The professor could begin to increase the homework assignment rate and perhaps examine its possible effect on the retention rate of the students. (Remember, however, that new control limits must be calculated when changes are made on the system.)

Other Control Charts

There are two other control charts that should be described, both of which can be useful in the academic setting. They are the **c-chart** and the **u-chart**. Like the np-chart and the p-chart, the c-chart and the u-chart test the stability of the system. Both are attribute control charts.

The c-chart and the u-chart measure the number of non-conforming items. The c-chart is used when the number of non-conformities is measured and the subgroup size is constant. The u-chart is used when the number of non-conformities is measured and the subgroup size is either constant or variable.

Since the preparation of the c-chart and the u-chart is similar to that of the np-chart and the p-chart, we will present briefly when and how the charts may be appropriately used.

c-chart

A c-chart is an attribute control chart that is useful when the characteristic under study is too complex for a simple yes/no, positive/negative answer. In other words, the data may have a number of discrepancies per subgroup. An example might include a purchase order form that is incorrectly completed because of errors in filling out the following:

- Vendor
- Vendor's address
- Vendor's telephone number
- Catalog number
- Item description
- Unit price
- Quantity ordered
- Total price
- Department cost code

(If you wanted to calculate the number of incorrectly completed forms regardless of which information item was done wrong, you'd use an np-chart; if you wanted to calculate the proportion of non-conformances regardless of which information item was incorrectly completed, you'd use the p-chart.)

As with the other control charts, you should perform the following tasks:

- Select the data to be analyzed
- Record the data
- Do the calculations
- Draw the chart
- Analyze the chart

Procedure

1. Select the data to be analyzed

Before using any control chart, it's essential that the operational definition of the non-conforming characteristics be carefully identified in order to insure consistency in the collection process. In the example below, the director of building and grounds, working with his crew, identified four major discrepancies in the "work order" requests that came to the department:

- The request was unclear.
- There was no approval signature by the supervisor.
- There was no cost code to which the work could be charged.
- There was no entry for the date on which the work was to be performed.

These entries were believed to be a major cause of work not being done in a timely fashion. They decided to examine a sample size of two forms at 8 a.m., 10 a.m., noon, 2 p.m., and 4 p.m. for five straight working days.

2. Record the data

Data for c-chart

(k) Subgroup #	Date	(c) # of Work Orders with Discrepancies
1	1/7	4
2		8
3		6
4		2
5		0
6	1/8	6
7		2
8		8
9		0
10		4
11	1/9	4
12		6
13		0
14		4
15		8
16	1/10	0
17		6
18		4
19		8
20		2
21	1/11	6
22		0
23		2
24		4
25		2
Total		96

3. Do the calculations

3.1   The **average number** is calculated according to the formula:

$\bar{c}$ = total number of unfilled requests ÷ number of subgroups
$\quad$ = C1 + C2 + C3 + ... + Ck ÷ k
$\quad$ = 4 + 8 + 6 + ... + 2 ÷ 25
$\quad$ = 96 ÷ 25
$\quad$ = 3.8

This number is placed at the top of the form next to "Avg."

3.2   The **Control Limits** are calculated according to the formulae:

$$UCLc = \bar{c} + 3\sqrt{\bar{c}}$$

$$= 3.8 + 3\sqrt{3.8}$$

$$= 3.8 + 5.8$$

$$= 9.6$$

$$LCLc = \bar{c} - 3\sqrt{\bar{c}}$$

$$= 3.8 - 3\sqrt{3.8}$$

$$= 3.8 - 5.8$$

$$= 0$$

4. Draw the chart

Do the scaling as described previously. In this case, the largest c number is 8 and the UCLc is 9.6. Therefore, take 9.6 and multiply it by 0.66 of the number of lines on your graph. In our case the number of lines is 30, and 0.66 of 30 is ≈ 20. Each line, in our case, has an incremental value of 9.6 ÷ 20 = 0.48. Adjusting upward, we have an incremental value of 0.5.

The completed c-chart is shown on the next page.

Completed c-chart

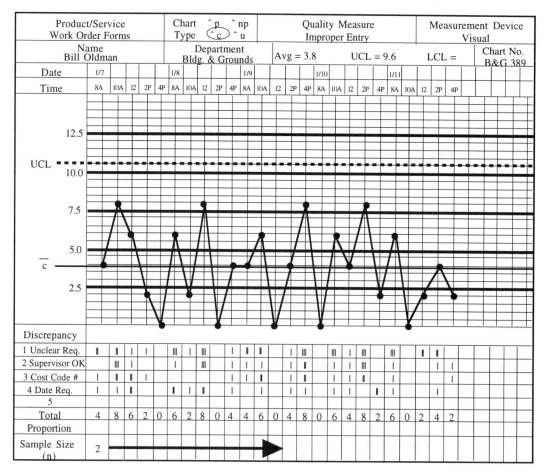

Product/Service Work Order Forms	Chart Type ^p ^np (c) ^u	Quality Measure Improper Entry			Measurement Device Visual
Name Bill Oldman	Department Bldg. & Grounds	Avg = 3.8	UCL = 9.6	LCL =	Chart No. B&G 389

Time	8A	10A	12	2P	4P	8A	10A	12	2P	4P	8A	10A	12	2P	4P	8A	10A	12	2P	4P	8A	10A	12	2P	4P
Date	1/7					1/8					1/9					1/10					1/11				

Discrepancy

1 Unclear Req.	I	I	I	I		III	I	III		I	II	I		I	III		III	I	III		III		I	I	
2 Supervisor OK		III	I			I		III		I	I	I		I	I		I	I	III		I		I	I	
3 Cost Code #	I	II	II	I						I	I	I		I	I		I	I	I		I			I	
4 Date Req.	I	I	II			I	I	I		I		I		I	I		I	I	II	I			I		
5																									
Total	4	8	6	2	0	6	2	8	0	4	4	6	0	4	8	0	6	4	8	2	6	0	2	4	2
Proportion																									
Sample Size (n)	2																								

5. Analyze the chart

The above chart does not demonstrate any special cause variation, because it doesn't go above the UCL. Therefore, the variability in the system appears to be due to common causes that can be reduced by improving the processes within the system. What eventually happened in this case was that the work order form was redesigned by an action team, and educational seminars on the proper procedure for completing the work order requests were conducted by the director of building and grounds for the department chairpersons, deans, and other unit heads. The increase in service and decrease in frustration levels were appreciated by all.

u-chart

A u-chart is an attribute control chart that is useful when the characteristic under study is too complex for a simple yes/no, positive/negative answer. In other words, the data may have a number of discrepancies per subgroup. An example might include an invoice form that is incorrectly completed because of errors in filling out one of many entries. (If you wanted to calculate the number of incorrectly completed forms regardless of which information item was incorrectly completed, you would use the np-chart; if you wanted to calculate the proportion of non-conformances regardless of which information item was incorrectly completed, you would use the p-chart.) However, unlike the c-chart, the u-chart can be used with either a constant or variable subgroup size. If the subgroup sizes vary by more than 25%, as demonstrated in our example below, individual control limits must be calculated.

As with other control charts, you should perform the following steps:

- Select the data to be analyzed
- Record the data
- Do the calculations
- Draw the chart
- Analyze the chart

Procedure

1. Select the data to be analyzed

Before using any control chart, identify the operational definition of the non-conforming characteristics to ensure consistency in the collection process. In the following example, the assistant vice president of administration, working with her employees, identified five major principle discrepancies that resulted in incorrect billing. (These were not listed in our example, but they would be scored in the same manner as shown for the c-chart above.) Redoing the bills was a major cause of rework and of failing to submit bills in a timely fashion, both of which caused "unhappy customers." The task force decided to examine a random number of invoices for 25 straight working days.

2. Record the data

The data are recorded as shown on the next page. (Note: the actual scoring for the five non-conforming characteristics is not shown. However, it should be done on your chart.)

Data for u-chart

Subgroup Day	# of Forms Examined	# of Incorrect Entries
1	3	8
2	4	16
3	5	12
4	5	4
5	4	0
6	4	12
7	3	4
8	2	16
9	5	0
10	4	8
11	7	8
12	5	12
13	4	0
14	4	8
15	3	16
16	2	0
17	3	12
18	5	8
19	4	16
20	7	4
21	4	12
22	4	0
23	4	4
24	4	8
25	4	4
Total	103	192

3. Do the calculations

3.1   The **average number per unit** ("Avg.") is calculated according to the formula:

$$\bar{u} = \sum c \div \sum n$$
$$= 192 \div 103$$
$$= 1.86$$

3.2   The **average subgroup size** is calculated according to the formula:

$$\bar{n} = \sum n \div k$$
$$= 103 \div 25$$
$$= 4.12$$

3.3   The **subgroup size limits** are calculated:

$$>25\% = 4.12 \times 1.25 = 5.15$$
$$<25\% = 4.12 \times 0.75 = 3.09$$

Therefore, any proportion number (in any subgroup) that is less than 3.09 or greater than 5.15 will have to have its UCL and LCL calculated separately. In our example, please refer to subgroups 1, 7, 8, 11, 15, 16, 17, and 20.

3.4   The **proportions** (u) for each subgroup are calculated according to the formula:
u = number in subgroup (c) ÷ subgroup size (n)

These figures are added to the chart.

3.5   The **control limits** are calculated according to the formulas:

$$UCLu = \bar{u} + 3\sqrt{\bar{u} \div \bar{n}}$$

$$= 1.86 + 3\sqrt{1.86 \div 4.12}$$

$$= 1.86 + 3\sqrt{0.4514}$$

$$= 1.86 + 3(0.6719)$$

$$= 1.86 + 2.02$$

$$= 3.88$$

$$LCLu = \bar{u} - 3\sqrt{\bar{u} \div \bar{n}}$$

$$= 1.86 - 2.02$$

$$= 0$$

3.6   The control limits for the subgroups that vary $\pm\ 25\%$ are calculated separately.

For subgroups 1, 7, 15, and 17:

$$UCLu = 1.86 + 3\sqrt{\bar{u} \div n} = 1.86 + 3\sqrt{1.86 \div 3} = 4.22$$
$$LCLu = 1.86 - 3\sqrt{\bar{u} \div n} = 1.86 - 3\sqrt{1.86 \div 3} = 0$$

For subgroups 8 and 16:

$$UCLu = 1.86 + 3\sqrt{\bar{u} \div n} = 1.86 + 3\sqrt{1.86 \div 2} = 4.75$$
$$LCLu = 1.86 - 3\sqrt{\bar{u} \div n} = 1.86 - 3\sqrt{1.86 \div 2} = 0$$

For subgroups 11 and 20:

$$UCLu = 1.86 + 3\sqrt{u \div n} = 1.86 + 3\sqrt{1.86 \div 7} = 3.41$$

$$LCLu = 1.86 - 3\sqrt{u \div n} = 1.86 - 3\sqrt{1.86 \div 7} = 0.32$$

4. Draw the chart

Do the scaling as described previously. In this case the largest proportion (u) is 8 and the UCLu is 1.86. Therefore, take 8 and multiply it by 0.66 of the number of lines on your graph. In our case, the number of lines is 30, and 0.66 of 30 is ≈ 20. Therefore, 8 ÷ 20 = 0.4 or ≈ 0.5.

Completed u-chart

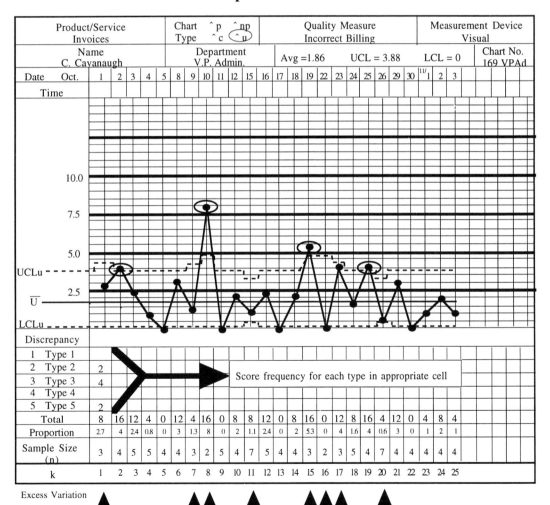

5. Analyze the chart

The chart indicates that the billing system is not in control. On October 2, 10, 19, and 25, the proportion of non-conformities exceeded the UCL, which indicates special cause variation. It was later discovered that two of the employees who were responsible for billing had serious health problems on those days that prevented them from performing satisfactorily.

FLOW CHARTS

Although flow-charting is one of the most useful tools in TQM, it is probably the most underutilized TQM tool in higher education. Flow-charting can help you get a snapshot of each process within a system. As a result, a **flow chart** can demonstrate where non-value-added work is performed. Of course, non-value-added work adds to the cost of doing business. In the case of higher education, this cost can be substantial.

When a flow chart is drawn and redundant processes are identified, a task force can easily generate a different flow chart showing how the processes within the system should be performed. It is essential when a flow chart of a system is drawn that everyone working within the system be involved in drawing it. At one university, the faculty hiring system includes no fewer than 30 processes and probably twice as many tasks before a candidate can be offered a contract. Until a flow chart was done, no one knew how cumbersome the hiring system really was.

There are many different types of flow charts, but we will describe two that are useful in academic units: the **deployment flow chart** and the **process flow chart**.

Deployment Flow Chart Procedure

1. Define the system

Each system consists of a series of processes. However, it's not always clear where one system ends and another begins, since many systems involve more than one department/unit. Take registration of students, for example. Each department is involved, as are the financial aid, parking, and housing units. Therefore, the task force should agree on the starting and ending points it wishes to study.

As with any universal tool, flow-charting has a set of standardized symbols (Myron Tribus, 1989). They are as follows:

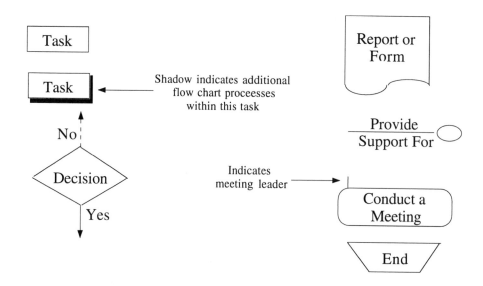

2. Draw the deployment flow chart

A deployment flow chart is useful when you want to show the relationships among people and the tasks they perform while working within a system to generate a service or product.

Before drawing a flow chart, the members of a task force should walk through each step in the system they are studying. As they do, they should ask the people performing each task what is actually involved in it. They should take copious notes and draw sketches. Flow charts should be drawn not only when there are problems within a system, but also when the system appears to be stable, in order to root out non-value-added work. Every task and process within every system should be flow-charted. In addition, if there are any changes within a system, its flow chart should be updated immediately for all to see.

The first thing you should do in preparing the deployment flow chart is to enter the **"people"** coordinate horizontally. The boxes can contain the person, his/her position, or the department/unit that is performing a task. In the example below, we'll follow the flow chart of a class schedule production system at a university.

Dean of Academic Affairs	Assoc. Dean of Academic Affairs	School Deans	Department Chairs	Clerk

Next, the actual tasks and/or major steps are listed:

1.   Prepare memo to proceed (dean of academic affairs, associate dean of academic affairs, and school deans) ⬭

2.   Analyze data (department chairpersons, school deans) ☐

3.   Generate schedules on spreadsheets (department chairpersons) ⬭

4.   Approve/revise schedules (school deans) ◇

5.   Compile data (dean of academic affairs and associate dean of academic affairs) ☐

6.   Enter schedules from spreadsheets into mainframe computer (clerk) ☐

7.   Check draft for errors (clerk, dean of academic affairs, associate dean of academic affairs, school deans, and department chairs) ☐

Using the symbols described above, draw the flow chart.

Dean of Academic Affairs	Assoc. Dean of Academic Affairs	School Deans	Department Chairs	Clerk

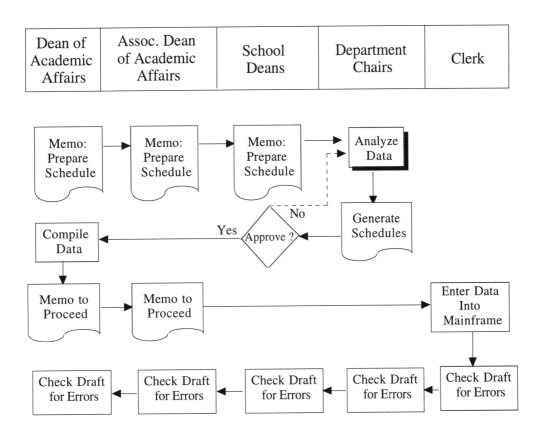

3. Record and discuss the results

Because the horizontal lines represent a customer-supplier relationship, the flow chart reveals the nature of the interactions. The flow chart must reflect **all** steps, even the illogical duplication brought about by system errors. You need to examine the lines and try to determine if there is any non-value-added work that can be reduced or eliminated. If there appears to be a breakdown in the system where someone is not supplying their customer with quality work, try to examine the reason(s) why. Are there barriers or decision-making delays that slow the flow?

In the above example, there were three memos to proceed with the process of producing the class schedule, two memos instructing the clerk to enter the data into the computer, and five separate checks for errors. This system actually existed within a university, yet numerous errors still existed in the final class schedule. Furthermore, by using the above-mentioned system, it took eight months to generate the schedule of courses.

A task force, after examining the system, recommended the revision shown below which not only reduced the time from eight months to eight days, but virtually eliminated all errors.

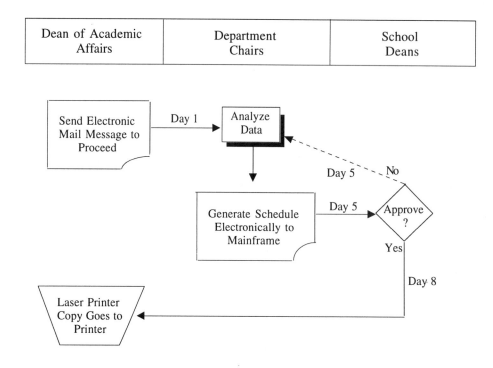

Process Flow Chart Procedure

1. State the problem

The process flow chart shows the major steps within a system. It doesn't attempt to demonstrate the interrelationships among the people doing the tasks. As with any flow chart, the task force should agree on the starting and ending points of the system it wishes to study.

2. Draw the flow chart

The members of the task force should take it upon themselves to actually walk through each step in the system they're studying. As they do, they should ask people performing each task what is actually involved. Copious notes should be taken, and sketches should be drawn. Only after this is done should the members draw the process flow chart.

The first thing to do in preparing the process flow chart is to list the major steps in the system. Then, using the standardized symbols shown below, draw the flow chart.

Using the example in the aforementioned deployment flow chart, you may have listed the major steps as follows:

1.   Send memos to proceed □

2.   Chairs analyze data □

3.   Chairs generate schedules □

4.   Approved? ◇

5.   Data compiled □

6.   Schedules entered into computer □

7.   Schedules OK? □

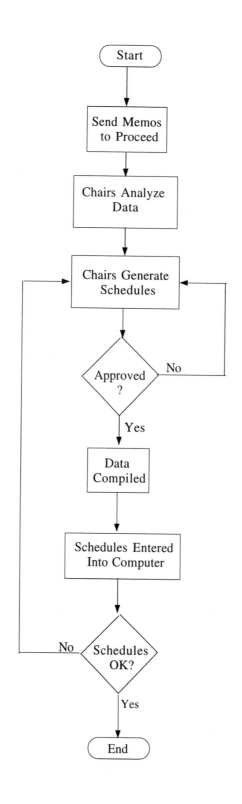

3. Record and discuss the results

By studying the flow chart, task force members can recommend ways to reduce redundant steps and improve the processes of the system.

FORCE FIELD ANALYSIS

The **Force Field Analysis** tool was the product of federally funded research to change the meat-buying habits of American homemakers during World War II. It was invented by Kurt Lewin of the University of Iowa.

Force Field Analysis helps a task force identify the perceived driving and restraining forces toward effecting a recommended change. Then, by increasing the forces driving the change or decreasing the forces inhibiting the change (or both), a task force can recommend actions to bring about the change successfully.

Actually, the Force Field Analysis is much more useful when used with other TQI tools (e.g., the **Nominal Group Process (NGP)**, **Affinity Diagram**, or **Scenario Builder**). This is especially true if the recommended change is counter to the "tradition" of the institution/department. Like the NGP, Affinity Diagram, and Scenario Builder, Force Field Analysis involves the use of proper brainstorming procedures: a facilitator is selected, team members have an equal opportunity to express their ideas without criticism, and the building of ideas is encouraged.

Procedure

1. State the problem

Under the direction of the facilitator, the members of the task force should arrive at a statement of the precise desired change they will suggest to management. To arrive at this statement, it may be necessary to use other TQI tools such as the NGP and the Affinity Diagram, as previously explained.

For example, a medium size, comprehensive, public university wanted to increase the number of minority students. It recognized the goal as a system problem (which was the perception in previously arranged NGPs) and clearly stated it as such.

2. Record the suggestions

After brainstorming on the driving and restraining forces (much like the procedure for the NGP), the task force — consisting of the president, the executive director of the local faculty union, faculty, and student representatives — recorded the perceived driving and restraining forces as shown on the next page.

FORCE FIELD ANALYSIS	
Recommended Change: Increase Number of Minority Students	
Driving Forces (+)	**Restraining Forces (–)**
	Limited number of minority students interested in our school
Administration, faculty and union interested in increasing minority enrollments	Not enough student aid and minority scholarships
Good working relationships with community colleges that have a high minority student population	No articulation agreements with community colleges to encourage minority transfers
	No minority programs to encourage minority students to stay
	No incentive for faculty to recruit minority students
Administration, faculty and union very interested in increasing the number of minority faculty	Very few minority faculty on-board to act as role models
	No minority organizations on campus
	No minority administrators

3. Discuss and prioritize the driving and restraining forces

The person who generates each idea should give his/her rationale on why he/she felt it was important. Then, an open discussion should be conducted on each point. Certain points could be combined under a single heading if the task force agrees. (Actually, the Force Field Analysis above is the final combined grouping that resulted when over 25 single entries were offered for both the driving and restraining forces.)

After discussion and grouping, the task force should assign a value of relative importance to each point. The values could be determined in a way similar to that in the NGP, where either a rank value or total points could be determined using a n – 1 numbering system. For example, eight separate points are listed in the restraining forces. Therefore, the group may wish to use the NGP technique and assign #7 the most important perceived restraining force, #6 the second most important, and so on.

In this case, the task force decided to use the NGP and the final ranking value (e.g., #1 was considered the most significant driving/restraining force [it received the most points], #2 the second most important, etc.). These values are placed next to the comments and are shown below.

FORCE FIELD ANALYSIS	
Recommended Change: Increase Number of Minority Students	
Driving Forces (+)	**Restraining Forces (−)**
	Limited number of minority students interested in our school (5)
Administration, faculty and union interested in increasing minority enrollments (1)	Not enough student aid and minority scholarships (6)
Good working relationships with community colleges that have a high minority student population (3)	No articulation agreements with community colleges to encourage minority transfers (4)
	No minority programs to encourage minority students to stay (8)
	No incentive for faculty to recruit minority students (2)
Administration, faculty and union very interested in increasing the number of minority faculty (2)	Very few minority faculty on-board to act as role models (1)
	No minority groups on campus (7)
	No minority administrators (3)

4. Recommend steps to be taken

After the driving and restraining forces are recorded, discussed, and prioritized the task force should recommend steps to effect the desired change. This should be done on the bottom of the form as shown on the next page.

The recommendations are now solidly based on documented observations and evaluation of the forces.

Force Field Analysis

Recommended change: Increase the number of minority students

Driving Forces (+)	Restraining Forces (−)
	Limited number of minority students interested in our school(5)
Administration, faculty and union interested in increasing minority enrollments (1)	Not enough student aid and minority scholarships (6)
Good working relationships with community colleges that have a high minority student population (3)	No articulation agreements with community colleges to encourage minority transfers (4)
	No minority programs to encourage minority students to stay (8)
	No incentive for faculty to recruit minority students (2)
Administration, faculty and union very interested in increasing the number of minority faculty (2)	Very few minority faculty on board to act as role models (1)
	No minority groups on campus (7)
	No minority administrators (3)

Recommended Actions:

1. The president should reward each department that hires a minority faculty member with additional funds and/or an additional faculty position. (This would address the top-ranked restraining force and the second-ranked driving force.)

2. Every department that increases its minority enrollment by more than 15% should be granted an increase in professional development funds. (This would address the second main restraining force.)

3. Chairs and deans should be encouraged to establish articulation agreements with the community colleges and build off-campus mentoring programs. (This would address the #4 and #5 restraining forces and #1 and #3 driving forces.)

4. Selection committees should encourage more minority faculty and administrators to apply for positions. (Addresses third-ranked restraining force.)

5. On-campus minority groups should be established.

From beliefs and values we get a set of proposed behaviors — policies — that with some certainty the team feels will be successful.

HISTOGRAM

The **Histogram** is a depiction of data on a bar graph representing how often a class of data occurs. One of the main purposes of using a Histogram is to predict improvements in a system or show results of system modifications. The system must be stable, however, or the Histogram cannot be used to make predictions. If the system is unstable, the Histogram might take different shapes at different times. Therefore, the Histogram is often used with a **Control Chart**.

A task force studying a system may gather statistical data about the system and draw a Histogram to help members assess the current situation. Then, in order to test a theory, the task force may change one or more processes within a system and, after gathering additional data and drawing another Histogram, check to see if the modifications improved the system.

The Histogram is used when you want to analyze the variation within a system. You must have a set of either related attributes (counts) data or variables (measurements) data. Although we will describe how a Histogram is prepared and how the shape of the Histogram may vary, we will not do the actual calculation of the statistics. Instead, we refer the reader to any elementary statistics book for the actual calculations.

In the example that follows, we have selected a case study from a chemistry department in which the chair demonstrated the benefits of the university investing in professional development money for the faculty. He made his case on the data he had accumulated from sending a particular professor to a workshop called "Teaching/Learning Styles: Increasing Student Success." Apparently, before 1990, only 25% of the students who took Professor Smith's "General Chemistry" class received a grade of "C" or better, while the remaining students received either a "D" or "F." The professor complained that students were lazy and could not be motivated to do better work.

The performance of Professor Smith's students on the chemistry department's standardized final exam reflected their final grades.

The chair suggested forcefully that perhaps Professor Smith could not teach (since he was apparently reaching only 25% of his class), and that perhaps he should examine his teaching style. Several semesters after Professor Smith took the workshop on teaching/learning styles, the chair, using Histograms, demonstrated the grade distributions on standardized tests of the students in Professor Smith's chemistry classes. The histograms are shown on the following pages.

Procedure

1. Select the data to be analyzed

We have assumed that the task force or the individual studying a system has already collected either the attribute data or the variable data. In this case, the chair of the chemistry department gave a standardized general chemistry proficiency exam after the students completed the course in either the fall or spring semester. He had data for how students performed in different classes with various professors.

2. Record the data

A frequency table is constructed, similar to those below, in which attributes data are recorded. In this case, the counts of tests scores are recorded by grade and frequency. Absolute frequency measures the actual number of each grade received. Relative frequency is the percentage of particular grades received. Relative cumulative frequency is the ongoing sum of the percentages of grades received up to, and including, any given level.

Frequency Distribution

Distribution of grades of the students from Professor Smith's classes
on the Chemistry Department's Proficiency Exam (CDPE), 1986-1989

Grade	Absolute Freq.	Relative Freq. (%)	Relative Cum. Freq. (%)
A	55	13.75	13.75
B	35	8.75	22.5
C	12	3.00	25.5
D	195	48.75	74.25
F	103	25.75	100
Total	400	100	

Frequency Distribution

Distribution of grades of the students from Professor Smith's classes
on the Chemistry Department Proficiency Exam (CDPE), 1990-1991

Grade	Absolute Freq.	Relative Freq. %	Relative Cum. Freq. %
A	52	26.13	26.13
B	89	44.72	70.85
C	49	24.62	95.47
D	7	3.52	98.99
F	2	25.75	100
Total	199	100	

3. Draw the Histogram

Starting with an x-axis (horizontal) and a y-axis (vertical) of approximately equal length (and of sufficient size to best display the data), the department chair began to draw a Histogram. He drew a bar for each "grade," with the corresponding "frequency" for which it occurred.

The resulting histograms show the distribution of grades of the students from Professor Smith's classes on the Chemistry Department Proficiency Exam (CDPE) from 1986-1989 (before the teaching/learning styles workshop) and from 1990-1991 (after the teaching/learning styles workshop).

**Distribution of grades from Dr. Smith's students
on the Chemistry Department's Proficiency Exam from 1986-1989**

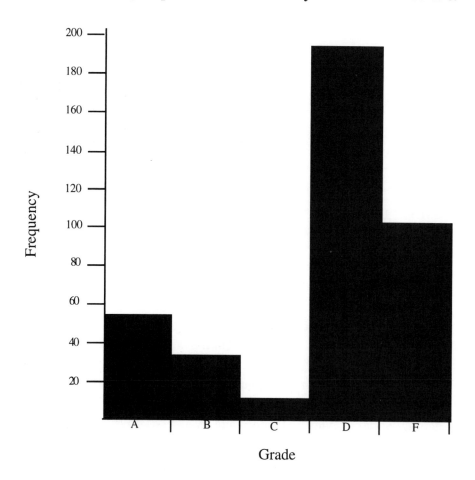

**Distribution of grades from Dr. Smith's students
on the Chemistry Department's Proficiency Exam from 1990-91**

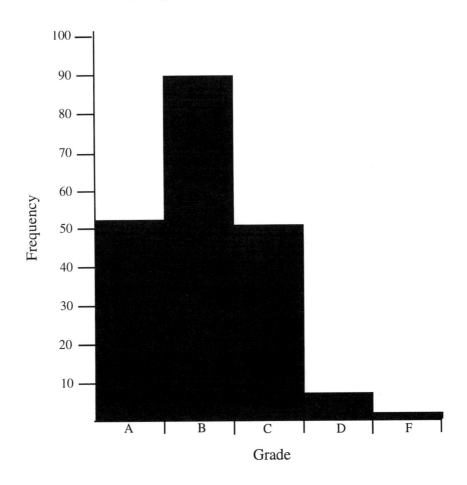

4. Analyze the shape(s) of the Histogram(s)

   Histograms have six common shapes: (1) symmetrical, (2) skewed right,
(3) skewed left, (4) uniform, (5) random, and (6) bimodal. These are shown on the following
page.

The Common Shapes of Histograms

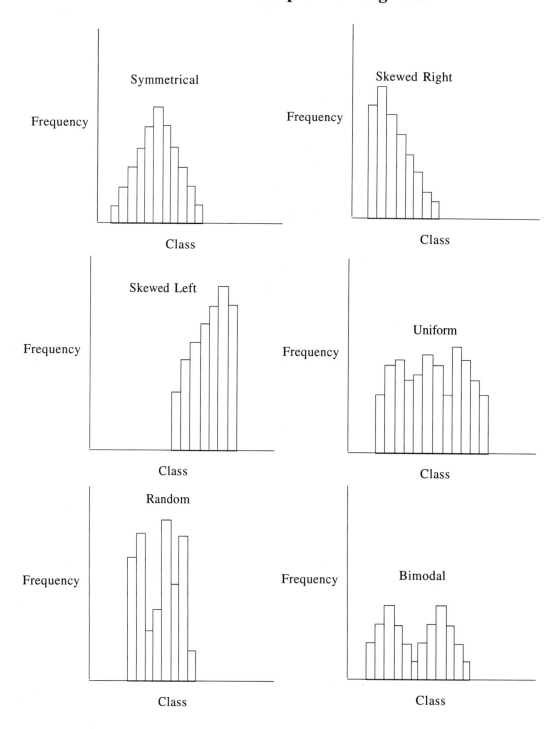

The symmetrical figure, also called a bell-shaped curve, usually represents a "normal" distribution, indicating that the system under investigation is probably under control. Ideally, the mean (average), mode, and median of the class data are equal, and 99.73% of the total area under the curve is plus or minus 3 standard deviations.

Histograms can also trail off either to the right or left. Whereas the skewing to the right is known as a positive skew, the trailing to the left is known as a negative skew. Both can occur when data have values greater than zero, as in our case study.

The uniform and random distributions can indicate that the system under investigation is out of control. By the same token, a uniform distribution may be the result of not having enough classes in your data, while the random distribution may result if you have multiple sources of variation in the system under study. In either case, these distributions usually provide little information.

The bimodal Histogram may indicate that the system under study is the result of several sources of data.

The first Histogram in our case study with Professor Smith's chemistry classes is either bimodal (two different peaks) or skewed left.

The bimodal shape might indicate that two different systems are operating and need to be separated and individually analyzed. (In this instance, you could make the case that Professor Smith did have two separate "systems" operating, namely, those students who were learning and those who were not learning. You could argue that Professor Smith had a teaching style that was compatible with approximately 20% of the students. If Professor Smith was able to learn in the very manner he was teaching, he might think that all students should be able to learn under similar conditions. He might consider those who did not pass his test as unmotivated or "dumb.")

The skewed left Histogram is "negatively skewed." It has a larger number of instances occurring in the upper classes (C – F) and few in the lower classes (A – B). As mentioned above, this distribution occurs when the data in a system have a possible zero point, and all the data collected have a value larger than zero.

The second Histogram is probably symmetrical. It has a bell-shaped curve. It may be a "normal distribution" in that it is symmetrical and within ±3 standard deviations, the percentage of data that fits under the curve is close to 100%. (In this case, you could make the case that Professor Smith was able to teach the majority of his students quite effectively, in that over 95% of his students received a grade better than "C" on the CDPE. It could be argued that Professor Smith had modified his teaching style so he could accommodate 95% rather than 25% of his students.)

The chair of the chemistry department, therefore, made the case for additional professional development money to retrain faculty in the differences between teaching and learning styles. The chair showed the difference in the cost of retaining students rather than recruiting new students to take the place of those who were suspended due to poor grades.

NOMINAL GROUP PROCESS

This technique is a structured process that helps the group identify and rank the major problems or issues that need addressing. This technique is also good for identifying the major strengths of a department/unit/institution. The technique gives each participant an equal voice.

The example below is taken from the College of Arts & Sciences at a rural, comprehensive public university. The session was called by the dean during the planning process. The chairs and one faculty member from each academic department were to arrive at a consensus about the perceived problems and/or weaknesses that inhibited quality.

For the **Nominal Group Process** (NGP), it is recommended that each group have a facilitator who is not part of the task force/unit. The facilitator may have to encourage some members of the team who are reluctant to contribute; likewise, the facilitator may have to restrain members who normally try to control such processes. All members need to feel comfortable with the process and with participating. Each facilitator will require a stopwatch during the workshop.

Each group should consist of five to 10 people. Since large units will have several groups, it's possible though unlikely that each group may perceive different problems/weaknesses. If this should happen, the facilitator may have to review the results and plan another session for the entire unit before the final ranking can be assigned.

Procedure

1. Introduce the process (5 minutes)

The facilitator provides instructions regarding the process but does not influence the group's decision. The facilitator keeps the group working within the time limits.

The facilitator tells the participants that the NGP allows them to explore areas systematically and arrive at a consensus. The process consists of developing a list and ranking perceived problems. The group discusses the results of the ranking and identifies the most important perceived problems.

2. Present the question (15 minutes)

The facilitator should direct the question to be considered to the group. For example, the facilitator, as in this case, might be instructed to ask the group: "What do you consider to be the major problem of your unit that is affecting quality?"

The facilitator should repeat the question and then ask each participant to write short and specific three-to-five-word answers for each perceived problem on Form A (see next page). The facilitator should request that each member complete Form A silently and independently, reminding the participants that they have five minutes for this task. At the end of five minutes, if it appears that several members have not finished, the facilitator should state that he or she will allow two additional minutes. If most members have already finished, the facilitator should not allow any extra time.

Form A
Listing of perceived problems
What do you think are the major problems in your unit that inhibit quality?
Please use the form below and write out short, specific answers.

Item #	Perceived Problem
1	
2	
3	
4	
5	

3. Develop a master list (20 minutes)

While the group is developing its list of perceived problems, the facilitator should use an overhead and project Chart 1.

At the end of the time allotted, the facilitator should ask the participants to stop writing. Then, in a round-robin fashion, the facilitator should ask each participant to read aloud one of the perceived problems on his/her list. If the group comes to a problem on the list that has been given, it need not be repeated. If one item is phrased differently from another but appears to be the same, group members may indicate by a show of hands whether they think the items are the same. If a majority feel the items are the same, the perceived problem should not be listed again; otherwise, both items will be listed. At this time, the facilitator may need to ask participants not to speak out of turn. There should be no discussion of the list at this point. For a period of time the participants should not be influenced (to avoid coercion) by the opinions or remarks of others. This must be adhered to early in the process. Otherwise, less assertive members will not raise problems that they alone might perceive (for instance, that another member likes to control department meetings). As each perceived problem is given, the facilitator should record the item on Chart 1. The facilitator must not suggest categories or combinations. The items should be numbered and recorded as presented by the participants without editing, unless the item is too long, in which case the facilitator could try to shorten the phrasing of the perceived problem without changing the meaning. If, at the end of 20 minutes, some group members have items that have not been presented, the facilitator should ask each member to give the one most important perceived problem remaining on his/ her list.

A sample of some of the perceived problems that resulted from the NGP in the College of Arts & Sciences is shown below.

Chart 1
Perceived problems that inhibit quality in the College of Arts & Sciences

Item Number	Perceived Problem	Sum of Initial Values	Sum of Final Values	Final Rank
1	Lack of facilities			
2	Insufficient sections of general education courses			
3	Dirty classrooms			
4	Not enough majors			
5	Large class sizes			
6	Untimely personnel plan			
7	Poor students			
8	Insufficient laboratory supplies			
9	Boss type managers (micro-management)			
10	Poor budgeting process			
11	Poor lateral communications outside of acad. aff.			
12	Uncommitted faculty			
13	Union-management relationship is poor			
n				

4. Clarify master list items (15 minutes)

The facilitator should point to each perceived problem on the master list and read the item aloud. The facilitator should ask if each item is understood. If an item is unclear, the facilitator should ask the individual who generated the item to address and clarify it. The facilitator should not condense the list or permit the group to discuss the relative importance of the perceived problems at this point. Remember, the purpose of this step is clarification.

5. Rank the items (15 minutes)

The facilitator should distribute Form B (see below) to each member of the group and should request that each member select and rank the five most important perceived problems of the unit. The most important perceived problem should be assigned a 5; the next most important item should be assigned a 4, and so forth. The participants then record their rankings on Form B, whereupon the facilitator should collect the forms and tally the results on the master list, giving each item an initial score.

Form B
Initial ranking of perceived problems
Please refer to the master list (Chart 1), which describes the perceived problems, and indicate in the table below what you think are the five major problems.

Item number from the master list	Initial subjective ranking value
	#5 (most important)
	#4
	#3
	#2
	#1 (least important)

Using the listings from the example in Chart 1, the members of the task force in the College of Arts & Sciences summed up respondents' values as well as the values respondents had assigned to each of the perceived problems.

Chart 1-a
Perceived problems that inhibit quality in the College of Arts & Sciences

Item Number	Perceived Problem	Sum of Initial Values	Sum of Final Values	Final Rank
1	Lack of facilities	13		
2	Insufficient sections of general education courses	33		
3	Dirty classrooms	2		
4	Not enough majors	21		
5	Large class sizes	23		
6	Untimely personnel plan	53		
7	Poor students	10		
8	Insufficient laboratory supplies	5		
9	Boss type managers (micro-management)	18		
10	Poor budgeting process	6		
11	Poor lateral communications outside of acad. aff.	1		
12	Uncommitted faculty	10		
13	Union-management relationship is poor	35		
n	Others	70		

6. Discuss rankings (30 minutes)

The facilitator should ask the participants to discuss the rankings. The participants may wish to **elaborate upon, defend,** or **dispute** the rankings. They may not add items. Items may be discussed even if they did not receive a high score. The members should be reminded that this is their opportunity to express opinions and persuade others.

At this point, similar items may be combined into a single category. In the above example, a total of 27 items was eventually reduced to nine.

7. Break (20 minutes)

The facilitator should encourage the participants to take a break and to move about, since it is rumored that if one sits too long, the blood drains from the brain to the lower extremities. Some members of the group may find this a welcome relief from the previous discussion (or debate, if that should occur). Others may want to take the discussion into the hallway. The facilitator should devise innovative means to have the members return promptly after the break is scheduled to end.

8. Create final listing and ranking of items (15 minutes)

After the items have been discussed the facilitator should distribute a copy of Form C (see below) to all group members. The facilitator should request each member to rank the top five choices as before: assign #5 to the item they consider most important; #4 to the second most important item, and so on. At the end of the allocated time, the facilitator should record the final values of each item on the master list.

Form C
Final ranking of perceived problems
Please refer to the revised master list (Chart 1), which describes perceived problems, and indicate in the table below what you think are the five major problems.

Item number from the master list	Final subjective ranking value
	#5 (most important)
	#4
	#3
	#2
	#1 (least important)

The results of the master list should be recorded and typed on Chart 1-b (on the next page). When this was done in the College of Arts & Sciences mentioned above, the following data were obtained.

Chart 1-b
Perceived problems that inhibit quality in the College of Arts & Sciences

Item Number	Perceived Problem	Sum of Initial Values	Sum of Final Values	Final Rank
1	Lack of facilities	13		
2	Insufficient sections of general education courses	33	114	1
3	Dirty classrooms	2	2	9
4	Not enough majors	21	4	8
5	Large class sizes	23	66	2
6	Untimely personnel plan	53	42	3
7	Poor students	10	13	6
8	Insufficient laboratory supplies	5	10	7
9	Boss type managers (micro-management)	18	13	5
10	Poor budgeting process	6	36	4
11	Poor lateral communications outside of acad. aff.	1	0	
12	Uncommitted faculty	10	0	
13	Union-management relationship is poor	35	0	
n		70	—	

OPERATIONAL DEFINITION

An **Operational Definition** is a very precise statement of what is expected from a given process. Many of the troubles within the academy probably result from imprecise or undefined objectives. Problems can also arise because Operational Definitions are unclear or vague. An Operational Definition is a prerequisite for collecting data and evaluating results, and everyone — members of the task force, faculty, secretaries, students — must clearly understand it.

Some examples:

- Students may want a clear definition of how their grades are going to be determined, including such simple and basic information as what they are expected to know when they complete a course, how they are to be tested, and what the classroom rules are.
- Faculty may misunderstand and fear post-tenure review processes. In some cases, the fears are well-justified, as such processes are often built upon quite shaky methodological grounds. Improperly designed pre-tenure review processes may actually work to undermine quality if they "drive in fear" (an allusion to Deming's Eighth Point, namely, "Drive out fear"). Faculty simply don't understand what is expected of them.

Operational Definitions are appropriate for every process or system that is to be improved, even though they may represent the actual objectives inaccurately. All members working on the process must accept a working definition, even if inaccurate, with the understanding that the definition is not set in stone. Most likely, any discrepancy in an operational definition results from changed conditions in the process. As the process is examined, the operational definition may have to be adjusted to suit the changed circumstances.

Procedure

Step 1: Establish specific improvement objectives

Consider the following hypothetical case. A biology professor has experienced a high failure rate when his students attempt the gram stain procedure. The biology chair has been tactfully suggesting for some time that the problem may not be with the students, but rather with the professor's teaching method. After the professor agrees that this may be the case, the two conclude that this is no time for blame. They agree that the professor's general objective should be to increase his students' success rate.

The professor, turning his back on the principles of natural selection that have governed his teaching style, decides upon the following Operational Definition: "I expect 95% of the students to correctly perform the gram stain procedure." Until now, 60% have succeeded at the procedure. To meet his Operational Definition, the professor will have to almost double the number of students who successfully complete the procedure.

Step 2: Define terms and conditions in the Operational Definition

Even though the professor has moved from the general desire to increase his students' success rates to the specific objective of almost doubling the number of students who succeed, he is still not quite ready to devise new teaching strategies to achieve his objective, because his Operational Definition presumes certain conditions and standards that must first be specified.

The professor's operational definition may, at first glance, appear fairly commonsensical. But the tricky phrase is "correctly perform." What does that mean, in the context of the professor's lecture-lab format? Before his students can "correctly perform" the gram stain procedure, the professor needs to identify three elements:

- the conditions for performance,
- the means for evaluating the performance, and
- a process for deciding whether the performance was successful.

For the first element — conditions for performance — the professor decides that students will be required to perform a gram stain on five unknown cultures of bacteria in the log phase of growth during a lab session. In addition, students will be given known cultures of gram-positive and gram-negative bacteria for their controls. (Of course, students will have been instructed previously — see below — on how to do the gram stain, and they will have performed it on several bacterial samples in order to develop proficiency prior to the lab test. In addition, the reagents will have been freshly prepared, the microscopes will be in good condition, and the professor will have distributed precise directions for doing the staining test.)

For the second element — a means for evaluating the performance — the professor will use standard biological procedures to determine whether or not students have identified each culture correctly.

For the third element — a decision process — the professor has to decide what proportion of cultures each student must identify correctly. In this case, he decides that students who correctly identify four out of five (or, of course, five out of five) have performed the task successfully.

Step 3: Alter the approach to the problem

Now that the professor knows precisely what he expects and what that means in specific terms, he can change certain parts of his teaching approach to try to achieve his Operational Definition. The professor decides to present the central instructional unit on the gram stain procedure using small groups led by TAs, as opposed to his traditional way of using a large lecture format. He maintains all other instructional conditions as before, as a control.

Step 4: Evaluate

The beauty of an operational expectation is that it provides a precise standard against which to measure subsequent performance. The professor alters his teaching method on gram stains, gives the precisely defined gram stain lab test, and finds that 90% of students have now succeeded (that is, they have identified successfully four or five out of the five cultures). That represents an improvement — evidence that the altered teaching strategy has worked — but still lower than the 95% the professor had specified in his Operational Definition. So the professor concludes that he is now on the right track, but he decides to make further changes in his gram stain teaching strategy.

You will appreciate why, given pressure from the chair, this professor might alter his Operational Definition or call for only 90% of the students to pass the staining procedure. If, for example, he were to define "correctly perform" as identifying only three out of five correctly, rather than four out of five, his students should, all other things being equal, demonstrate a significantly higher success rate. They would no doubt be pleased, as would their professor, but such a nominal increase in the success rate would be built upon the proverbial "watered-down standards," clearly anathema to a TQI environment. The biology chair will need to learn how to keep fear out of his workplace in order to encourage this professor to maintain high academic standards.

PARETO DIAGRAM

The Pareto Diagram is a TQI tool that is used to identify the few significant factors that contribute to a problem and to separate them from the many insignificant ones. It is based on the work of Vilfredo Pareto, an Italian economist (1848-1923). It was made popular by Joseph Juran in the 1940s. However, it was Alan Lakein who came up with the 80/20 rule of the Pareto Diagram — that is, about 80% of the problem comes from about 20% of the causes.

The Pareto Diagram is a simple bar chart with the bars arranged in descending order from left to right. Although many consider it a problem-solving tool, it is really best for guiding a team to the problem areas that should be addressed first.

In the example below, we've selected a case study from a university where requests for renovation and repairs (known as "work orders") in the division of buildings and grounds were not being completed in a timely fashion. Many of the repairs were not accomplished simply because the "work order" form was not completed correctly. The maintenance staff identified six categories that attributed to the majority of errors:

- Unclear requests
- Supervisor's signature absent
- Unit cost code absent
- Date on which the work was to be performed absent
- Location of renovation/repair not specified
- Work order request misfiled

The director of building and grounds appointed a task force and asked members to collect and analyze the data. As part of their study, the team members used the Pareto diagram, shown below.

Procedure

1. Select the categories to be analyzed

The members of the task force should identify the data they must collect to address a particular problem (time, location, number of defects and errors, etc.), and place them into a category. Keep the number of categories to 10 or less.

2. Specify the time period in which the data will be collected

Obviously, the time period you select will vary according to the system under study. It may be hours (as with the time it takes accounting to cut a check) or years (as in the case of testing an improvement theory). However, the time selection should be constant for all diagrams being compared.

In the example, the director chose to compare the six categories over the past academic year.

3. Record the data

You need to construct a table with a category column and a frequency column, as shown below.

Category	# of Violations
Unclear requests	130
No supervisor's signature	74
Cost code absent	46
Date to perform absent	40
Location not identified	38
Work order misfiled	32
Total	360

Construct the frequency table, showing the category, frequency, relative percentage, cumulative occurrences, and cumulative percentage.

Category	Number of Occurrences	Relative Percentage	Cumulative Occurrences	Cumulative Percentage
Unclear request	130	36.1	130	36.1
No supervisor's signature	74	19.7	204	55.8
No cost code	46	12.8	250	68.6
Date to perform	40	11.1	290	79.7
Location not identified	38	10.6	328	90.3
Work order misfiled	32	8.9	360	99.2
Total	360	99.2%		

4.   Draw the graph

You need to draw the x-axis (horizontal). It should be long enough to best display your graph and may vary from a few inches to six or seven inches. The width of each bar should be equal. In the case study, the x-axis of 3.6 inches was selected, and the scaling factor of 0.60 inch was selected to represent each of the categories.

Draw two vertical lines (y-axes) of equal length, as shown below. They should be as long as the x-axis, if not longer. Again, they should be long enough to best display your graph.

Label and scale these axes. In this case study, the x-axis will represent the categories being compared, the y-axis on the left will represent the number of occurrences, and the y-axis on the right will represent cumulative percentage.

Starting the Pareto Diagram

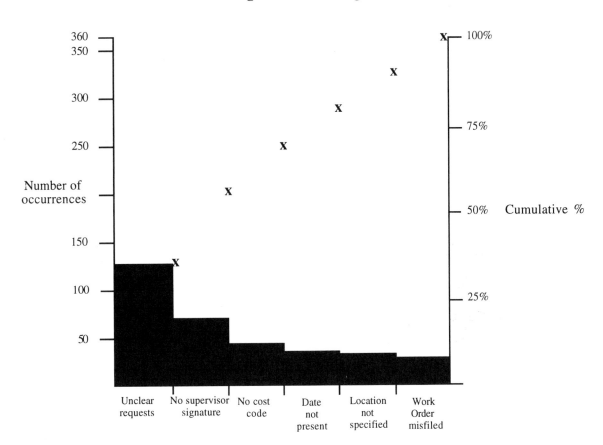

After you draw the graph, you need to plot the cumulative frequencies and draw a line connecting the marks (**x**), as shown on the next page.

5. Analyze the diagram

It is not unusual for 80% of the problem to be caused by a few categories, and the Pareto Diagram will easily demonstrate this. In the above example, over 55% of the occurrences were due to the first two categories.

You must be careful when using this powerful tool. It is true that the Pareto Diagram can point out chunks of data that can be used by a task force to analyze causes and direct efforts toward a few categories. But there are data that cannot be easily categorized. Some data, without further analysis, may be misleading if they are too general. The aforementioned data could be misinterpreted if the director simply concentrated on the first two categories.

Finished Pareto Diagram

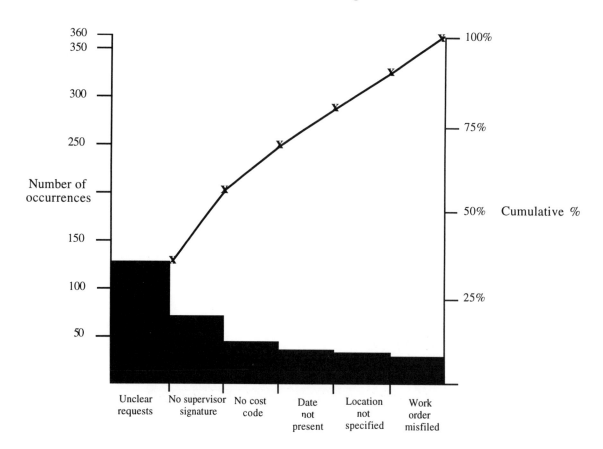

The director analyzed the data further by constructing another Pareto Diagram of the first category (unclear request). This time, he plotted the number of unclear requests with the administrative units submitting the requests (as shown on the next page).

Administrative Unit	Number of Occurrences
1	0
2	5
3	5
4	5
6	10
7	50
8	30
14	25

From the data, the following frequency table was constructed as described above.

Admin. Unit	Number of Occurrences	Relative Percentage	Cumulative Occurrences	Cumulative Percentage
#7	50	38.5	50	38.5
#8	30	23.1	80	61.6
#14	25	19.2	105	80.8
#6	10	7.7	115	88.5
#2	5	3.9	120	92.4
#3	5	3.9	125	96.3
#4	5	3.9	130	100.2
#1	0	0	130	
Total	130	102		

The number of work orders with unclear requests, by administrative unit

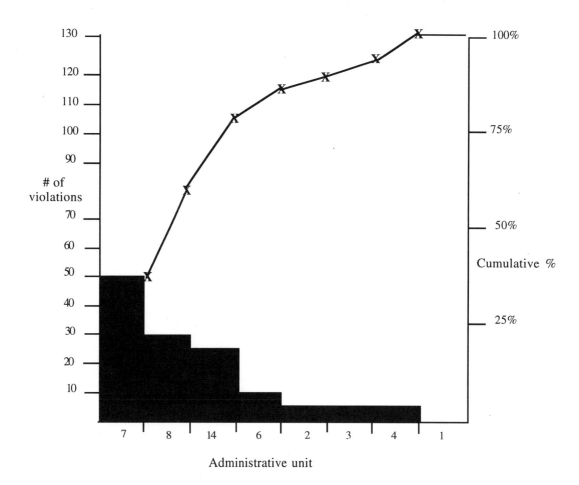

When examined closely, the Pareto Diagram and the corresponding data indicate that the greatest number of unclear requests were from administrative unit 7. Furthermore, analysis showed that Pareto's rule applied: roughly 80% of the problems stemmed from just administrative units 7, 8, and 14. The concentration represents an unequivocal sign to administrators to focus first on those three units.

RELATIONS DIAGRAM

The **Relations Diagram** is used as a planning tool. It is rarely used alone. When used with either the **Scenario Builder** or the **Affinity Diagram**, the Relations Diagram is a powerful tool to arrive at root causes and effects of a process or a problem.

When a task force uses the Relations Diagram to examine a complex problem over an extended period of time, it will most likely be able to direct its efforts toward the major root causes of the problem(s) in an efficient manner. It will also be able to constantly update and modify the necessary actions that might result from observed changes in the system under study.

Procedure

1. State the problem

Although it is possible to use the Relations Diagram by identifying a problem/issue and then stating it in a brief and specific manner, it is much more efficient to examine a complex problem/issue with other tools before using the Relations Diagram. It's best that the task force first utilize one of the other tools (the **Nominal Group Process** or the **Affinity Diagram**), to arrive at a consensus on the process/issue under investigation. Only then should the team analyze the findings further with the **Relations Diagram**.

The example below followed a session with the chairs in a school of technology. The dean and faculty at the school were attempting to start a new degree program in TQM. Since the college was under considerable financial constraints, it was difficult to obtain optimistic support from other areas of the college. After doing an analysis with an Affinity Diagram, the team posted the following header cards for the question, "What are the issues associated with us establishing a new B.S. degree program in TQM?"

1. Develop and do a needs survey
2. Demonstrate need to the Vice President for Academic Affairs
3. Get support of the curriculum committee
4. Get the support and input of regional businesses
5. Get support of college faculty
6. Develop a curriculum
7. Develop and implement informational activities

In order to arrive at the root causes and effects of the issue, the chairs and deans next constructed a **Relations Diagram**. This is shown on the next page.

2. Record the perceptions

Place the header cards from the Affinity Diagram in a circular pattern around the problem/issue being examined, as shown below. This can be done on an overhead projector, but a large sheet of flip chart paper is usually better.

Starting the Relations Diagram

```
                  ┌──────────────┐
                  │  Develop &   │
                  │ Implement    │              ┌──────────────┐
                  │ Informational│              │Develop & Do a│
  ┌──────────────┐│  Activities  │              │ Needs Survey │
  │  Develop a   │└──────────────┘              └──────────────┘
  │  Curriculum  │
  └──────────────┘

  ┌──────────────┐   ╭──────────────────────────╮   ┌──────────────┐
  │ Get Support  │  ╱ What are the issues associated╲ │ Demonstrate  │
  │ from College │ │  with us establishing a new BS  │ │ Need to VPAA │
  │  Faculty     │  ╲ degree program in TQM?       ╱  └──────────────┘
  └──────────────┘   ╰──────────────────────────╯

       ┌────────────────┐          ┌────────────────┐
       │  Get Support &  │          │ Get Support from│
       │Input from Regional│        │ the Curriculum  │
       │   Businesses    │          │   Committee     │
       └────────────────┘          └────────────────┘
```

3. Demonstrate inter-relationships

You might ask whether there is a cause-and-effect relationship between the header groups. In the example below, the task force decided that it was necessary to develop and do a survey in order to get support and input from regional businesses. As a result, the task force drew arrows away from the cause and toward the header that the cause would affect or influence.

The inter-relationships were continually examined until all headers were compared to each other. When the task force finished this, they constructed the final version of the Relations Diagram, shown on the next page.

Inter-relationship on the Relations Diagram

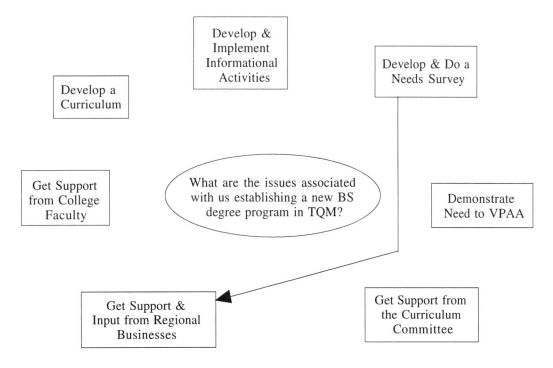

Completed Relations Diagram

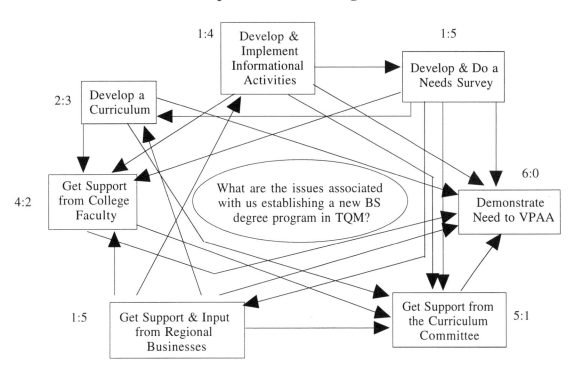

4. Analyze the inter-relationships

Count the number of arrows that are directed toward each header and the number departing from each. Express this as the ratio "#Toward : #From." Write each ratio next to its respective header, as shown above.

The root causes are those headers that have the greatest number of arrows going From; the root effects are those headers having the greatest number of arrows going Toward. In the above example, the two root causes suggest that the task force should conduct a needs survey and get the support of the regional businesses, in order to have positive effects on the curriculum committee and the VPAA.

To demonstrate the power of this simple tool, look at the section on the Affinity Diagram. When the task force from this institution did a Relations Diagram on the Affinity Diagram's headers, it obtained the following result:

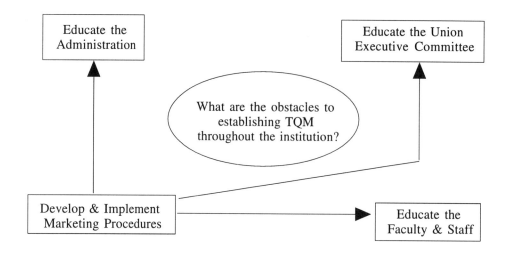

The results were clear: Before TQM could be implemented at this institution, the task force would have to implement marketing procedures for the administration, faculty and staff, and the Union Executive Committee. (Actually, the initial "marketing procedure" was simply to conduct education workshops.)

RUN CHART

A **Run Chart**, also called a Tier Chart, is a line graph of data in which the observed values can be either measurements (variables) or counts (attributes). The data is plotted on the vertical axis while the time is plotted on the horizontal axis.

One of the main benefits of a Run Chart is that it allows you to examine the functioning of a system over time. Similar data plotted together in a Histogram may not reveal an important trend in the system that could require corrective action.

A Run Chart is constructed from data that is collected as the system is in operation. It is often used by a task force as the initial tool in gathering information about the system under study. Usually, more than 25 points are required for a valid Run Chart.

A Run Chart is a simple TQI tool and can be used with a wide variety of data. Run Charts are useful for a single snapshot or for following trends. Various units within an academic institution could make excellent use of Run Charts by posting good and poor trends for all to see and analyze. (Note: These charts should never be used as a threat, or employees will refuse to offer their suggestions for how the system can be improved.) Depending upon the data, the time factor can be seconds, minutes, hours, days, weeks, or years. Depending upon the data, it may be possible to add the statistical Upper Control Limit (UCL) and Lower Control Limit (LCL) and make the Run Chart a Control Chart.

Procedure

1. Select the data to be analyzed

We have assumed that the task force or the individual studying the system has collected either the attribute (counts) data or the variable (measurements) data. In the case study below, we will examine the average final grade of students in the introductory course in "Computer Sciences" as a function of the MWF class periods over five semesters. The courses were taught by six different professors, but they all used the same syllabus and textbook.

2. Record the data

Record the data in the order in which it was collected (as shown on the next page).

**The MWF average final grades (by year and semester)
in the "Introductory Computer Sciences" classes
over the five semesters from 1988 to 1990**

Class Period & Time MWF Class Period	YR 1 1st	YR 1 2nd	YR 2 1st	YR 2 2nd	YR 3 1st
#1 (8-8:50 a.m.)	86%	88%	84%	85%	82%
#2 (9-9:50 a.m.)	86%	87%	89%	85%	85%
#3 (10-10:50 a.m.)	80%	80%	79%	88%	88%
#4 (11-11:50 a.m.)	80%	81%	79%	80%	82%
#5 (12-12:50 p.m.)	79%	72%	84%	83%	79%
#6 (1-1:50 p.m.)	80%	83%	83%	79%	81%
#7 (2-2:50 p.m.)	71%	65%	69%	74%	71%
#8 (3-3:50 p.m.)	66%	66%	72%	75%	64%
#9 (4-4:50 p.m.)	72%	72%	76%	71%	70%
#10 (5-5:50 p.m.)	78%	88%	84%	81%	84%
#11 (6-6:50 p.m.)	96%	97%	91%	90%	98%
#12 (7-7:50 p.m.)	93%	98%	92%	89%	91%

3. Draw the chart

You must first scale the chart; this will vary depending on the type of data collected (variables or attributes).

In scaling for the variables data, start by finding the largest and smallest values in the data. In our case, the largest was 98% and the smallest was 65%. The difference between these are determined (98 - 65 = 33). A rule of thumb for producing readable graphs with sufficient space above the highest value is to count the number of lines on your graph paper and multiply it by 0.66. The chart paper used in our case study has 30 lines; therefore, 30 x 0.66 = 19.8, or approximately 20. The graph will use about 20 lines.

The chart should be carefully labeled, as shown below:

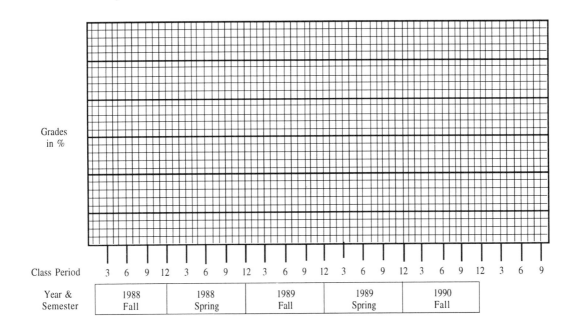

Divide the difference between the largest and smallest figures in your data set (33% in our case study) by two/thirds the number of lines on your chart paper (20 in our example); 33÷20 = 1.65, or approximately 2. Therefore, the increment value of the lines on our chart will be set at 2%.

Next, the lines should be numbered from the middle of the chart. Since our values range from 65% to 98%, the value that is approximately one half the difference is 16. The center number will thus be the low value + the difference between the high and low values, or 65% + 16. Since the total equals 81%, we will set the center line at 80% and assign an incremental value of 2% to the other lines.

Scaling for attributes data is identical to that of the variables scaling, except that the first line of the chart is assigned a value of zero and the increment values were added from the bottom up.

The data points are plotted on the graph paper and the points are connected with straight lines. These are shown in the two examples on the next page.

A run chart of the MWF average final grade of the introductory "Computer Sciences" classes over the five semesters from 1988 to 1990

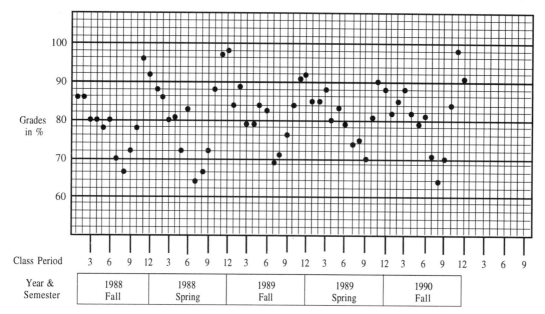

A run chart of the MWF average final grade of the introductory "Computer Sciences" classes over the five semesters from 1988 to 1990

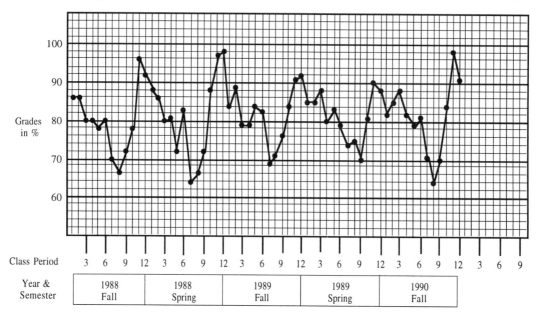

4.   Analyze the chart

Look for runs of seven or more points (see the explanation of "run" in the Control Charts section), as well as for other patterns.

In our case, it was discovered that the highest grades were in class periods 11 and 12, regardless of who taught. In these late-evening classes, the students consisted mainly of older, working, married, goal-oriented students who were taking one class at a time for either a degree or for personal advancement. The lowest grades were in periods 7 and 8, the mid-afternoon classes. Again, it did not appear to make any difference which professor taught the classes. Later it was revealed that these periods had the highest rate of absence. As a result, a peer and faculty mentoring program was established, and students received a call every time they missed a class; over the next several semesters we were informed that it appeared the students in the afternoon classes were performing as well as those in the morning classes.

SCATTER DIAGRAM

Scatter Diagrams are used to test the possible inter-relationships of two factors. If a relationship appears to exist, you can say that the factors are correlated. However, a cause-and-effect relationship can be verified only with the use of Control Charts. A Scatter Diagram is useful for analyzing causes of poor processes or systems.

Procedure

1. Select the data to be analyzed

In the following case study, a department chair wanted to test whether the mid-term grades of the students in a freshman mathematics course were related to class size. She wanted to test the proportion receiving a "D" or lower grade (including "D," "F," "I," or "W") to the class size during the fall quarter. (Note: While a minimum number of 25 pairs of data is desirable for an appropriate analysis, the actual case study presented here has only 22 samples.)

2. Record the data (as shown on the next page).

Course MA105 Section #	Class Size	Proportion with Grades ≤ D
001	25	.080
002	27	.074
003	30	.100
004	30	.133
005	30	.133
006	30	.200
007	30	.167
008	30	.167
009	30	.133
010	25	.040
011	25	.080
012	32	.156
013	36	.083
014	36	.194
015	36	.167
016	45	.222
017	45	.244
018	50	.300
019	50	.180
020	36	.139
021	55	.273
022	55	.309

3. Draw the diagram

The first thing you should do is scale the diagram so that both axes are approximately the same length. The length of the axes should be enough to accommodate your entire range of values, and the entire length of each axis should be utilized. In our example, the class sizes ranged from 25 to 55, so we made each marker on the x-axis 0.5 inch. The x-axis usually contains the data believed to be the influencing, or independent, factor, while the y-axis contains the dependent, or responding, factor. In our example, the chair believed that larger class sizes resulted in little interaction with the students and were the cause of poor grades. Therefore, the independent factor is class size, and the dependent factor — that which responds to the independent factor — is the proportion of midterm grades of D or less.

The diagram should be labeled and dated, and the points should be plotted. The completed diagram is shown below:

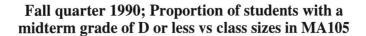

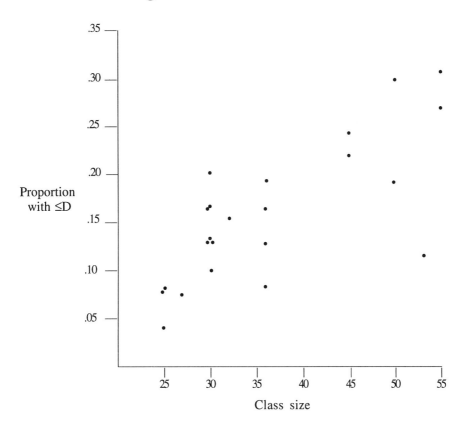

4. Analyze the diagram

Although it looks like there might be a positive correlation between class size and the proportion of students who received a grade of "D" or less at midterm, there were many other factors that influenced the grades. Further analysis by an action team using other TQI tools discovered that the time of day the classes were offered and the number of absences in the classes were the major causes of poor grades. The team also found that class sizes had little to do with the grades students received in this particular math class. This example is included here to warn you about potential misinterpretation of data that appear to be correlated but have other underlying factors.

SCENARIO BUILDER

The **Scenario Builder** is a planning tool that roughly quantifies the outcomes that may result if one or more proposed changes to a system are implemented. It is useful for analyzing the most likely outcomes of a change to a complex system. A tool that asks, "What if?", the Scenario Builder concentrates the efforts of team members on proposing the most likely outcomes, both positive and negative. It is a powerful tool that combines many of the features obtained from the Affinity Diagram, Nominal Group Process (NGP), Force Field Analysis, and Systematic Diagram. Like the Affinity Diagram, it attempts to organize complex issues; like the Nominal Group Process, it forces the group to identify and rank the most likely effects that the proposed change may bring; like the Force Field Analysis, it concentrates on both the positive and negative driving and restraining forces, and the action steps that should be taken to overcome the resistance of implementing the change. Finally, like the Systematic Diagram, it helps identify possible action items that are necessary to implement a broader goal.

The Scenario Builder should not be used until the task force members are familiar with the Affinity Diagram, NGP, Force Field Analysis, and Systematic Diagram. The Scenario Builder is no replacement for the aforementioned tools, but it is a tool to consider if the situation under examination has required two or more of the other tools for elucidation. Although the Scenario Builder requires a minimum of three hours of concentrated effort to complete, it still may save the task force many hours if, for example, three TQI tools would be required to arrive at similar conclusions.

Procedure

1. Spell out the recommended changes

Before using the Scenario Builder, the group should have already defined the system that requires modification. In fact, the team members should have solidified the change(s) that must be implemented in order to improve the system. The task force members should stipulate that the appropriate recommendations will be accepted to implement the change.

The recommended change ("**C**") is placed in the middle of the hexagon (see next page).

2. Record the perceptions

The task force members should list at least three beneficial outcomes of the proposed change and, if possible, three undesirable outcomes of the proposed change on the chart on the following page. The three beneficial outcomes should be listed in the squares labeled 1 through 3; the three undesirable outcomes should be listed in squares 4 through 6. (Sometimes it is difficult or almost impossible to identify three truly unacceptable outcomes as a result of implementing improvements in processes or systems. However, the group should attempt to identify at least two undesirable outcomes.)

Scenario Builder to determine the effects of change

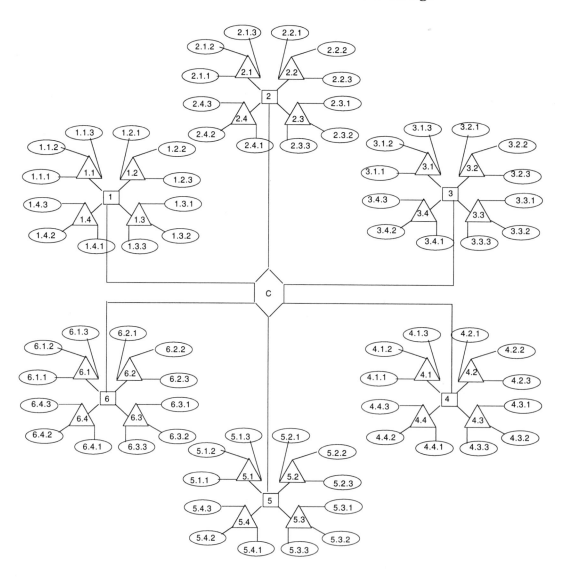

Following the above pattern, the group should label four scenarios that are likely to occur as a result of the outcomes identified in squares 1 through 6. If possible, two scenarios should be positive and two should be negative. In any event, at least one should be either positive or negative. These scenarios correspond to the four triangles that branch off from each square in the figure.

The aforementioned pattern should be repeated with the ellipsoids, which we'll label "results of scenarios." At least one of these results should be either positive or negative at any of the levels.

3. Score the scenarios

Scoring of the scenarios can be done either as they are listed or afterwards. But all six first-level outcomes (represented by the squares) should have at least a 70% perceived probability of occurring. To score the Scenario Builder, the group assigns a number of +1 to +10 to any positive outcome that might occur if the change is implemented, and -1 to -10 to any negative outcome that might occur. For example, the group may decide that a positive outcome, A, identified and placed in square 1, would surely result if the change were effected, and, thus they assign a value +10. The +10 means that the positive scenario would occur 100% of the time if the change were implemented and **if** nothing were done to stop it.

Likewise, a +3 should be assigned a value of 30%; +4 a value of 40%, and so on. The group may decide that positive outcomes B and C should be assigned values of +7 and +5, respectively. Similarly, the task force might decide that negative outcome D would almost definitely occur (100% of the time) if the change were implemented; therefore, they would assign it a value of -10, whereas the negative outcomes E and F would only be assigned values of -3 (30%) and -4 (40%), since they are less likely to occur if the change is implemented. If a very positive scenario would occur if the change is effected, and if its effect could not be altered, it should be assigned a value of +50. Likewise, if a disaster would occur if the change is implemented, and if its effect could not be altered, it should be assigned a value of -50.

The values for the first-level outcomes, 1 through 6, should be recorded on a Scenario Builder tally sheet as shown below. Likewise, the values for the second-level scenarios, 1.1 through 6.4, should be recorded. Finally, the values for the third-level results, 1.1.1 through 6.4.3, should be recorded. The scoring guidelines for the scenario builder are shown below.

Scenario Builder Tally Sheet

Positive Scenario	Negative Scenario	Percentage of the Time Scenario Would Occur	Effect Can Be Altered?
+1	-1	10%	Yes
+2	-2	20%	Yes
+3	-3	30%	Yes
+4	-4	40%	Yes
+5	-5	50%	Yes, Requires Effort
+6	-6	60%	Yes, Requires More Effort
+7	-7	70%	Yes, Requires Much Effort
+8	-8	80%	Yes, with Difficulty
+9	-9	90%	Yes, But Unlikely
+10	-10	100%	Not Likely
+50	-50	100%	Never

4. Interpret the scores

The team should examine the first-level outcomes, labeled 1 through 6, and they should have values ±7 (all should have a greater than 70% chance of occurring if the changes are implemented). If they do not, the action team should ignore them.

The task force should continue to build upon the **major** positive and negative projections through levels 2 and 3. It should concentrate on projections with values of ±7 or greater.

5. Describe what will likely happen for each outcome and then what action step needs to be taken to accentuate the positive and minimize the negative outcomes

With the identification and ranking of both positive and negative outcomes that would result from the implementation of the task force's recommendations, action steps can now be identified to either recommend the change and minimize the possible negative outcomes or abandon the change if projected negative outcomes suggest such a change would be disastrous.

6. List and analyze any scenario that has an absolute value greater than 100

When hypothetical projections have high scores, it usually means that if the recommended changes were implemented and if the perceptions of the task force members were representative of the institutional culture, then the projections would actually take place (moving from the hypothetical to the real if the change were implemented).

7. Suggest one or two systems that should be improved to maximize the positive and minimize the negative

Scenario Builder Tally Sheet

1. _____	1. _____	1. _____	1. _____
1.1 _____	1.2 _____	1.3 _____	1.4 _____
1.1.1 _____	1.2.1 _____	1.3.1 _____	1.4.1 _____
1.1.2 _____	1.2.2 _____	1.3.2 _____	1.4.2 _____
1.1.3 _____	1.2.3 _____	1.3.3 _____	1.4.3 _____
Total _____	Total _____	Total _____	Total _____
2. _____	2. _____	2. _____	2. _____
2.1 _____	2.2 _____	2.3 _____	2.4 _____
2.1.1 _____	2.2.1 _____	2.3.1 _____	2.4.1 _____
2.1.2 _____	2.2.2 _____	2.3.2 _____	2.4.2 _____
2.1.3 _____	2.2.3 _____	2.3.3 _____	2.4.3 _____
Total _____	Total _____	Total _____	Total _____
3. _____	3. _____	3. _____	3. _____
3.1 _____	3.2 _____	3.3 _____	3.4 _____
3.1.1 _____	3.2.1 _____	3.3.1 _____	3.4.1 _____
3.1.2 _____	3.2.2 _____	3.3.2 _____	3.4.2 _____
3.1.3 _____	3.2.3 _____	3.3.3 _____	3.4.3 _____
Total _____	Total _____	Total _____	Total _____
4. _____	4. _____	4. _____	4. _____
4.1 _____	4.2 _____	4.3 _____	4.4 _____
4.1.1 _____	4.2.1 _____	4.3.1 _____	4.4.1 _____
4.1.2 _____	4.2.2 _____	4.3.2 _____	4.4.2 _____
4.1.3 _____	4.2.3 _____	4.3.3 _____	4.4.3 _____
Total _____	Total _____	Total _____	Total _____
5. _____	5. _____	5. _____	5. _____
5.1 _____	5.2 _____	5.3 _____	5.4 _____
5.1.1 _____	5.2.1 _____	5.3.1 _____	5.4.1 _____
5.1.2 _____	5.2.2 _____	5.3.2 _____	5.4.2 _____
5.1.3 _____	5.2.3 _____	5.3.3 _____	5.4.3 _____
Total _____	Total _____	Total _____	Total _____
6. _____	6. _____	6. _____	6. _____
6.1 _____	6.2 _____	6.3 _____	6.4 _____
6.1.1 _____	6.2.1 _____	6.3.1 _____	6.4.1 _____
6.1.2 _____	6.2.2 _____	6.3.2 _____	6.4.2 _____
6.1.3 _____	6.2.3 _____	6.3.3 _____	6.4.3 _____
Total _____	Total _____	Total _____	Total _____

SYSTEMATIC DIAGRAM

The **Systematic Diagram** is a planning tool for determining the specific action steps that are necessary to accomplish a broader goal, especially if a number of people/departments/units are involved. It is usually not used alone but with an Affinity Diagram or a Relations Diagram.

Procedure

1. State the problem/goal

We will build upon the example presented in the Relations Diagram section. A task force consisting of the dean and a group of faculty in the School of Technology was attempting to establish a Bachelor of Science degree program in TQM. The goal is drawn on the left side of the paper. This can be done using an overhead projector or a large sheet of flip-chart paper.

End
```
┌──────────┐
│ Establish │
│  a B.S.   │
│  in TQM   │
└──────────┘
```

2. Generate levels of events and actions necessary to accomplish the end

The first level of events and actions is usually broad, but as you move from left to right, the tasks become very specific. One level builds upon the other. In the example that follows, the task force knows that it will ultimately need approval from the chancellor's office and support from the president, vice president of academic affairs (VPAA), and the College's Council of Trustees if it is to accomplish its goal. In order to gain that approval, however, the task force recognizes that it will require support from the academic deans, curriculum committee, and faculty senate. It will also need to develop a curriculum, do a needs survey, and obtain support from regional businesses. The various steps are spelled out in the completed systematic diagram at the end of this chapter.

3. Analyze the diagram and assign tasks

After the systematic diagram is completed, the task force members should analyze their findings and discuss them with members of their department/unit. Then, specific tasks or action steps with specific time lines should be assigned. In fact, it's a good idea to post the Systematic Diagram with the names of the people responsible for accomplishing a specific task.

The cynical reader may object that this Systematic Diagram presumes agents within a system can be both means and ends in the TQI process. In the aforementioned case, the cynical reader asks, is it fair to assume that, once the faculty senate has gained approval of the VPAA, he or she will then necessarily become a committed advocate for the recommended change? What if the VPAA gives nominal approval, but deep down remains uncommitted or even negative about the recommended change? Such a VPAA could very well sabotage the process by presenting it to the president in such a way that, while apparently its advocate, he or she is actually its assassin. Such a VPAA would bear out Hamlet's observation that "one can smile and smile and still play the villain." And, needless to say, such a VPAA would prove a highly effective saboteur of TQI.

There is no easy answer to this question. We have constantly stated that TQM and TQI must be continually talked up at all institutional levels, relying on Deming's principles that organizations must first "improve constantly" and "involve everyone in the transformation." Obviously, much more work needs to be done at an institution such as the one where the cynical reader resides.

Establishing a B.S. in TQM: Systematic Diagram

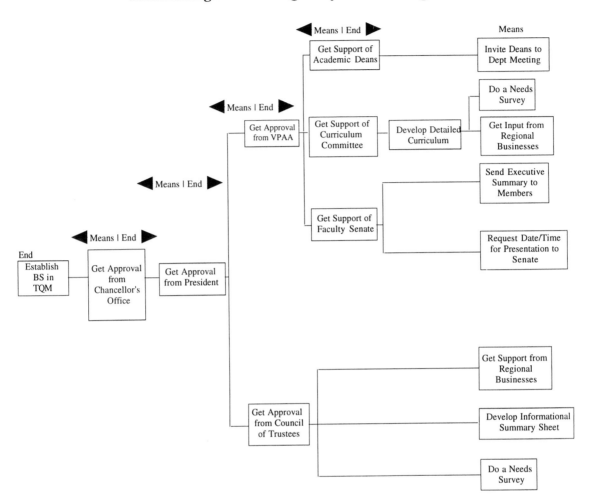

REFERENCES

Cornesky, Robert A., *et al.* (1990), *W. Edwards Deming: Improving Quality in Colleges and Universities*. Madison, WI: Magna Publications, Inc.

Cornesky, Robert A., Sam McCool, Larry Byrnes, and Robert Weber (1991), *Implementing Total Quality Management in Educational Institutions*. Madison, WI: Magna Publications, Inc.

Crosby, Philip (1984), *Quality Without Tears: The Art of Hassle-Free Management*. New York: McGraw-Hill Book Co.

Deal, T.E. and A.A. Kennedy (1982), *Corporate Culture*. Reading, MA: Addison-Wesley.

De Man, Henri (1939), *Joy in Work*. Trans. Eden and Cedar Paul (from German). London: George Allen & Unwin.

Deming, W. Edwards (1982), *Out of the Crisis*. Cambridge, MA: Productivity Press or Washington, DC: The George Washington University, MIT-CAES.

Gardner, John W. (1993), *On Leadership*, New York: The Free Press.

Glasser, William (1990), *The Quality School*, New York: Harper Perennial.

Imai, Masaaki (1986), *Kaizen: The Key to Japan's Competitive Success*. Cambridge, MA: Productivity Press.

Juran, J.M. (1988), *Juran on Planning for Quality*. New York: Free Press.

Levering, Robert (1988), *A Great Place to Work: What Makes Some Employees So Good, and Most So Bad.* New York: Random House, Inc.

Manz, Charles C., and Henry P. Sims, Jr. (1990), *Superleadership*. New York: The Berkley Publishing Group.

Peters, Thomas J. (1987), *Thriving on Chaos: Handbook for Management Revolution.* New York: Knopf.

Quehl, Gary H. (1988), *Higher Education and the Public Interest: A Report to the Campus*, Washington, D.C.: Council for the Advancement and Support of Education.

Waterman, Robert H. (1990), *Adhocracy: The Power to Change*. Knoxville, TN: Whittle Direct Books.

APPENDIX

The Development of a Formula-Driven Budget
John R. Bolte, Ph.D.
Vice President for Administration & Finance
University of Central Florida

THE DEVELOPMENT OF A FORMULA-DRIVEN BUDGET

John R. Bolte
Vice President for Administration & Finance, University of Central Florida

In order to drive a long-range plan, institutions may find it helpful to design a formula-driven budget that reflects the action objectives of the plan. Note, however, that formula-driven budgets can be improperly designed and used. Care must be taken to avoid certain pitfalls as described by Deming's Point #11: "Eliminate quotas and numerical goals; substitute leadership." This piece describes commonly used budgeting processes and outlines the development of a properly designed and tested formula-based budgeting procedure.

In recent years, the concerns of accountability, leveling or decline in enrollments, and availability of computerized management information systems in higher education have focused attention on the need for more precise and sensitive methods of providing appropriate internal allocation of resources. Simultaneously, the control of internal resources in educational institutions, particularly resources used by the academic areas, has shifted to individuals who are most directly involved in the use of the resources. Active involvement of academic resource-users and decision-makers in the allocation process has made the development of realistic allocation models possible. It has also placed additional responsibilities on offices of institutional research where data to support the allocation process should be available.

The budgeting and allocation of personnel and financial resources are both time-consuming and costly. Further, the number of procedures used to request and allocate resources is apparently limited only by the number of post-secondary institutions in existence. Procedures range from complex and ill-defined requests and allocation methods involving several administrative levels to singular, if not dictatorial, decisions on resource allocation. Budget requests and allocation procedures also range from those requiring mountains of paperwork, historical data, and rambling justifications to allocations that are purely formula-generated and based on some general variable such as student-credit-hour productivity.

The development and use of resource allocation models must be looked upon as a management tool. It is not a substitute for decision-making. Used properly, the resource allocation model reflects policy decisions of university administrators, provides information for short- and long-range planning, and has a substantial and desirable impact on the decisions made by deans and department chairs in the day-to-day operation of an educational institution. Used improperly, an allocation model may become a substitute for decision-making and result in decisions that are not in the best interest of the institution. In addition, a model not built on a firm rational basis places the academic administrator in a continually defensive position and may create morale problems with resource users. Because the resource allocation model requires more planning and analysis on the part of academic decision-makers, it facilitates an equitable and consistent allocation of available resources.

The comments that follow summarize a variety of procedures used in requesting and allocating resources and describe some of the limitations and advantages of each. The list in no way exhausts the various procedures used, but it does describe general categories that will be recognized singularly or in combination as an approximation to the procedures used in most institutions.

1. The Blue Sky Request

Most university budget officers, as well as top- and middle-level administrators have at one time or another been involved in a budget process in which unit heads with budget responsibility have been asked to submit a listing of their budget needs for a subsequent year, complete with written justifications for each item. Refinements include requiring that requests be listed in priority order and placing a limit on total dollars requested. Regardless of the constraints placed on such requests, budget officers can usually expect to receive personnel requests 2-5 times higher, and financial requests 5-10 times higher than even the most optimistic observers would predict for available resources. The corresponding justifications for the resources range from meaningful to senseless. Only occasionally do they provide sufficient information for the inevitable judgments that must be made when the actual budgetary resources become known and available. The results of this budget approach are easily enumerated and generally negative:

- High expectations of unit heads fail to materialize, and over time these individuals become demoralized or find the whole process to be something of a bureaucratic joke.
- The process offers little in the way of guidelines for inevitable cuts in the budget requests: Did each unit head inflate his or her request equally? Should the writers of a well-written and innovative justification be rewarded?
- The volume of paperwork and extent of staff, faculty, and administrative effort required to produce a budget request can be enormous.
- In what may be a more positive vein, input to the budget process seems to involve many people. At least, many people have had the opportunity to think about and provide input to the budget process even if their chances of receiving the requested funding are slim or nonexistent.

However, if the planning process described in this approach is used, people will have had a great deal of input in determining the goals and objectives of their units. If the purpose of resource allocation is to drive the plan, then both faculty and administrators will have had input into the allocation.

Overall, the Blue Sky budget request and allocation procedures waste time, deal in non-realities, and lower the morale of participants who (at least initially) may take the system seriously.

2. Planned Programmed Budgeting

Planned Programmed Budgeting, as the name implies, requires the development of a budgeting plan for the future. In a college or university, plans would be developed in each major program category and would include cost estimates and budget requirements to complete the stated plan. Budget managers expect to receive the required funding and, in turn, are expected to complete the stated plan within the approved budget. Unfortunately, college administrators are not known for their success in long-range planning and are even less adept at establishing realistic cost estimates for the tasks required by a plan. A complex combination of inabilities to do long-range planning, estimate student demand and enrollment by discipline, and estimate program or project costs tends to render Planned Programmed Budgeting useless at this time in most colleges and universities.

3. Zero-Based Budgeting

Zero-Based Budgeting implies that during each budget cycle the various budgetary units begin by assuming they have no continuing resources and that the new budget must be developed with statements and justifications for each activity requiring funding. The task can be long and laborious, but budget managers soon learn to use a previous year's budget request, adjusting dates appropriately and raising all budget figures by an amount 2-5% greater than the highest inflation estimate currently available. Additional amounts are then added to fund new programs deemed to be desperately needed or to fund existing programs that have obviously been under-funded (although successful) for several years. The procedure is supposed to force each budgetary unit manager to review needs and priorities periodically and thereby prevent outdated or inefficient programs from being continued.

Colleges and universities, however, are people-intensive, and any significant change in priorities or workload will impact personnel. A downward change may be compounded by the fact that some personnel are tenured, and administrators have limited flexibility to reduce or terminate programs. In the final analysis, Zero-Based Budgeting in its true form is probably never used in colleges and universities; what is often used is a modified procedure in which some fixed baseline continuing funding is established as zero base, and all expenditures in excess of this figure are specifically requested and justified. In either case, the system requires extensive and detailed documentation by administrators and budget managers. Unfortunately, the documentation can seldom be used effectively when actual budgets are received and internal allocations made.

Colleges and universities operate under remarkably stable conditions in terms of workload and funding. Variations in excess of 10% in any one year are exceptions and almost always predictable. From a budgeting point of view, it cannot, therefore, be said that major variations in workload or funding will significantly affect internal priorities for budgeting and allocation of resources in the short term. But such variations will affect budgeting and allocation of resources over 3, 5, and 10 years.

With reasonably stable and predictable resources and with the equally reasonable assumption that internal priorities do not change radically over short periods of time, the internal allocation of resources can be accomplished in a much more efficient and systematic manner, even if the purpose of the allocation is to drive the long-range plan. There is no apparent reason for unit administrators to request and justify budgets in advance. It makes little sense to have individual unit managers compete for reasonably fixed and limited resources through time-consuming and generally unsuccessful request and justification procedures.

A more rational approach is to devote time and effort during the mid-year lull in the annual budgeting cycle to establish and agree upon allocation procedures regardless of total funding received and in light of the goals of the institutional long-range plan produced. Such procedures can always be reduced to mathematical formulations that are easy to understand and efficient to use. The development of such a system has a number of advantages:

- The procedure provides ample opportunity to involve affected administrators and budget managers in the allocation process.
- It emphasizes the equitable allocation of available resources rather than Blue Sky requests and detailed justifications for non-existent funding.
- After funding is known, allocations can be made quickly and with few hurried decisions.
- Implementation of, and changes in, short- and long-range plans are still possible but in a more realistic context for estimating available resources. Total workload and financial resources are predictable with reasonable accuracy, and good estimates of future funding in a college or department become possible using the established allocation procedures, even if the allocations are used to implement change.
- Special program emphasis over a sustained period is possible by establishing predetermined favorable allocation parameters known and understood by those receiving added support as well as those who do not receive such support. Actually, these allocation parameters come from the institution's long-range plan.

Of course, not all internal resource allocations can be handled by the formula approach described above. There are often legitimate and justifiable reasons for short-term special allocations. For example, new programs may require start-up funding, an expensive research instrument may be needed, matching funds for a significant grant or donation may be required, or an expenditure that will benefit all budgetary units may have merit. There seems to be no established rule for the amount of funds that should be administratively reserved for special requirements. In institutions of higher education, it is probable that administered special allocations should be equal to or less than 1% of the total institutional budget. Administered special allocations in an institution of 10,000 students with a $50 million budget would then amount to as much as $500,000 across all budgetary units. At best, however, the 1% figure is a rule of thumb. It will depend to some extent on internal problems and future planning needs as viewed by high-level administrators. If drastic changes for the institution are anticipated over the next few years, 5-10% of the budget may have to be placed in the special allocation category.

A number of factors play a role in the development of successful allocation resource models. Regardless of the kind of resources being allocated or complexities in the use of available resources, the following factors apply:

- The model must reflect the goals in the institutional long-range plan and the corresponding policy decisions.
- The model must reflect actual resource use.
- The model must be based on factors that are general.
- The model must be more complex and detailed when resources are allocated close to the administrative level where they will be used.
- The model must be adaptable to mathematical formulation that is easily understood by the resource user.

A key requirement in developing and using a resource-allocation model is that the model must reflect previously established institutional goals and policy decisions, as reflected in the long-range plan. More important, the model must be designed and stated so that it encourages the attainment of institutional goals. For example, an allocation model might reflect an institutional goal to emphasize and build a strong Fine Arts program by providing favorable allocation parameters in this area. Similarly, if institutional administrators feel strongly that faculty travel to professional meetings is important to the growth and development of the institution, the allocation model should specifically identify professional travel as an allocation category. In austere times it may be necessary to increase class sizes in selected areas. It may be a goal to establish part-time, evening degree programs to reach the atypical, older, married, goal-oriented student population. Again, the allocation model should reward endeavors along these lines. Likewise, the institution may desire to reward department "joint ventures" with industries, and the allocation procedure could reflect positively on such innovations. (Under no circumstances should an allocation procedure stifle creativity, innovation, or academic freedom.) Such decisions, once made and clearly stated, should be reflected in the allocation model.

It is crucial that institutional goals and policy decisions as reflected in the long-range plan be known or established prior to developing and using an allocation model. Allocation models cannot, and do not, make decisions. Allocation models provide a concise, efficient, and understandable method of allocating resources only after basic goals and policy decisions are established. Gaining knowledge, insight, and commitment regarding institutional goals is often the most difficult phase of allocation model development; as a result, the prior development of the long-range plan becomes critical.

A successful resource allocation model must be clear and reflect planned uses of the resources. If faculty members are expected to teach, do research, and counsel students, then these factors should appear and be used in the allocation model that generates faculty positions. If faculty are to be encouraged to teach evenings and weekends, and/or to generate income for the division of continuing education, then different factors become important. If a certain category of funding is for expendable items, then these items should be categorized into suitable groups that can be identified in the allocation model. The appropriate reflection of use is essential if the model is to be credible and accepted by those who receive the allocated resources.

An interesting but unacceptable procedure used in developing a resource allocation model deserves some comment. In this procedure, an array of historical data points establishes a regression equation used to make subsequent allocations. Although regression equations can be useful in model development, the final allocation model must not be based solely on historical allocations nor on equations that, to the non-statistically oriented resource user, have no clear justification. Unfortunately, historical resource allocations sometimes reflect continuing inequities in allocations rather than a rational approach to resource allocations.

A successful resource allocation model must use general allocation factors. It is necessary to consider broad categorical needs for most resources to be allocated. Allocation models must be viewed as averaging techniques that guide the decision maker in the allocation process, and, therefore, they should not be sensitive to highly specific and detailed needs. Specific and often minor requirements of the resource user are a part of special allocations that the decision-maker may choose subjectively. They should not be allowed to clutter the allocation model. In reviewing an allocation model with those who use the resources, there is always the tendency to get into a discussion of detailed needs which are believed to be unique to a particular discipline. As an example, if faculty allocations are based on classroom and laboratory student-credit-hour production, a department chair will often begin to identify course by course differences in required faculty time and effort. A chair may also be greatly concerned about a factor such as the inexperience of his or her faculty and will claim that the model does not take into account the fact that inexperienced faculty must carry a lighter student/credit-hour load. Some of these concerns may be valid, but an allocation model that attempts to include excessive detail invariably fails, for one or more of the following reasons:

- Factors included in the model normally must be predicted several months in advance, and detailed factors usually are difficult to predict .
- Detailed or minor factors are often manipulated by users, who realize that the factors influence allocated resources. They tend to overemphasize these factors in their own decision-making.
- Including detailed or minor factors in a model usually causes all resource users to be preoccupied with discovering still additional factors which are unique in their discipline and which should be included in the model.

In summary, each factor that seems to play a role in allocation needs must be weighed carefully to see whether it is a significant factor of general concern to both the administrator and the users or if it can be more effectively and properly "averaged" into existing factors.

For those who are particularly enthusiastic about using an allocation model to allocate available resources to implement a long-range plan, the temptation to include additional complexity and detail in the model can be overwhelming. Further, the resource user who always sees his or her area or discipline as unique continues to encourage recognition of isolated factors that will divert greater resources to the area. To be realistic, however, the administrative model user must include detail in an allocation model only to the extent that the particular administrative level has knowledge of the use of the resources. It makes no sense, for example, for a legislature, a board of trustees, or an academic vice president to be concerned about the amount or type of chemicals needed in the chemistry department. The board of regents overseeing several large universities has little reason to try to determine and allocate variations by discipline in funding for faculty travel to professional meetings or in the monies to be spent for adjunct faculty members as opposed to regular faculty members, unless, for example, part of the institution's long-range plan is to increase part-time, evening enrollments by using part-time faculty.

In more concrete terms, a legislature providing funding for a large state university system should use an allocation model that has but one or two factors. The legislature would probably be interested in the total number of FTE students served as the major parameter in providing funding and might identify a few special projects that would be funded for relatively short periods of time. Because education is people-intensive, the legislature might also place constraints on the use of funds by limiting the amount of the total allocation to be used for employing personnel. This would prevent over-commitment to salaried personnel in future years.

The board of regents or state department of education that receives legislative funding would be concerned with more detail. Here, allocation model parameters would identify individual institutions and would probably retain FTE students as a factor. But they might recognize differential funding for students at the undergraduate and graduate levels; at the part-time, evening, minority level; and, at the full-time, day, traditional level. The governing board might also choose to allocate available funding in broad areas such as instruction, research, libraries, and physical plant maintenance. In so doing, the authority and level of control over resources at the local university level would be somewhat reduced.

At individual universities, the vice president for academic affairs (VPAA) would use a still more complex allocation model. The VPAA may choose to emphasize teaching, research, and service differently among the disciplines represented at the university and may recognize differing costs in laboratory disciplines. In addition, the VPAA may wish to encourage off-campus instruction in one or two areas. The allocation model at this level should contain a significant amount of detail compared to the model used by a state legislature.

The successful resource allocation model must be developed so that it can be reduced to mathematical formulation. Regardless of the kind of resource to be allocated, both the factors controlling the allocation and the resources allocated are ultimately numerical quantities which, no matter how difficult, must be related mathematically. Any other alternative requires that the allocation be made subjectively. Although one expects the administrator to make a limited number of allocations based on subjective decisions (perhaps as little as 1% or as much as 10% of the total allocation), stability of the system requires that most of the allocation be made more objectively.

A mathematical formulation of a model permits both the allocator and the user to state clearly the allocation procedure. Each can predict future allocations by estimating anticipated workloads and total resources and examining the long-range plan. It also becomes possible to assess quickly the effects of small changes in a well-established model when proposed changes are being considered. This is critical if significant change is desired in the short term.

A resource allocation model must actively involve those who will use or reallocate available resources. This involvement must center on the rationale for resource allocation and not on the quantity of the resource which any given model will produce. Little is ever accomplished in developing or modifying an allocation model if the discussion centers on the resources to be received by the user. Predictably, such discussions always result in a favorable response from those who will receive increased resources and disapproval by those who will receive fewer resources.

Development of a resource allocation model should be initiated by someone who knows the availability and the use of resources and who is intimately involved in the allocation process. Factors related to the resource needs are easily identified, and it often becomes a function of the office of institutional research to gather data on how expenditures have occurred in the past. Although historical data should not control resource allocation model development, the data can give clues to appropriate allocation factors as well as to past allocation inequities, especially in light of the goals in any new long-range plan.

The following steps are normally required to establish a new allocation model:

1. At the institutional level, someone with budget responsibility, working with the office of institutional research and the long-range planning document, must take the initiative to determine allocation factors and parameters which appear to be significant in the allocation of funds to the various subunits under the administrative office where the allocation model is to be used.

2. Through discussion with levels of administration above that in which the allocation model is to be used, an attempt must be made to determine policies, goals, and objectives of the administrative leadership that would influence budgetary policy. The long-range plan with its written goals and specific objectives, will help clarify major administrative desires for budgetary emphasis.

3. Discussions with resource users and with levels of administration below those where the model is being developed are essential to determine how the users view their needs and major resource requirements in light of the long-range plan. It is this group that will be most impacted by the model, and its input is crucial if the idea is to succeed.

4. A written document outlining the allocation model must be prepared. The document must include both the rationale of the allocation procedure and the specific procedure by which the allocation will be made.

5. The written document must be reviewed and approved, in principle, by the higher administrator or administrators who are ultimately responsible for the resource allocation that will implement the long-range plan.

6. The written document must be reviewed by administrators and resource users who will receive the resources.

This last step is of prime importance in the development of a satisfactory allocation model. These individuals must provide, by one means or another, the final rationale for the allocations to be made, and they must have reached reasonable accord that the model will acceptably distribute the available resources if change is to occur successfully. This process will require a considerable amount of time and effort and is, in fact, an ongoing process as the model undergoes change and refinement each year as subtle changes occur in the long-range plan itself. Resource users must participate in the LRP review process, since the success of the allocation model ultimately depends on understanding and acceptance by all who are affected by the evolutionary changes in the institution and by the resources allocated. In addition, it is essential that users wrestle with alternatives to the model if they are to understand and appreciate the complexities of budgetary allocation.

Some examples of the formula-based resource allocation model

The examples presented below suggest an allocation process that might be developed in an office of academic affairs.

Example 1: The allocation of faculty positions

The development of an allocation process requires discussion of factors directly related to the need for a particular type of resource. Once these factors are determined, questions of priority and importance of each factor must be considered and evaluated. Naturally, disagreements will occur. It becomes the task of higher-level administrators to review the arguments presented and develop acceptable compromises.

Questions that might be raised in the development of an allocation process for faculty positions include the following:

- What tasks are required of a typical faculty member?
- Are these tasks equally distributed and required across disciplines or do disciplines differ significantly in the need to perform the tasks identified?
- What factors determine the need for faculty positions in each task identified?

A number of conclusions about the need for faculty positions might be reached after review and discussion by deans and department chairs. For example, these administrators would quite probably conclude that the major need for faculty positions is for instruction with important additional needs in the areas of research, creative activities, student counseling, service on university committees, and administrative tasks. They might also conclude that research and creative activities are important faculty activities in all academic departments and that the distribution of research and creative activities positions should be based on the size of the department.

Further discussion might suggest that the number of positions for instruction should be based on the number of students served, recognizing that average class sizes, and therefore, the number of faculty needed, will differ among disciplines. For example, a department that typically teaches classes in the lecture mode will need fewer faculty positions for a given number of students served than will the department that must teach a majority of classes in a laboratory setting. The discussion might center on class sizes that would permit an acceptable level of quality in the instructional process.

Of course, it must be recognized that resources are finite. Sooner or later, acceptable class sizes in each discipline have to be stated. When this is done and when other factors that are considered important have been identified, an explicit statement of the allocation process can be made. A general description of the faculty allocation model might include the following major categories for allocating faculty positions:

1. An allocation of faculty positions for instruction based on the anticipated student/ credit-hour load in each discipline. The expected average student/credit- productivity per faculty member allocated would be different depending on the particular discipline under consideration and might differ depending on whether the instruction was at the lower, upper or graduate levels.

2. An allocation of faculty positions for academic counseling. This allocation might be dependent on the number of student majors being served or on specific discipline-dependent counseling needs. (The number of foreign students or the number of minority students who might require additional counseling could affect the needed faculty positions for counseling.)

3. An allocation of faculty positions for research, creative activities and service, including work on university committees and off-campus non-instructional activities.

4. An allocation of faculty positions allocated by the office of academic affairs, including department chairs, assistant deans, and graduate program coordinators.

In actual use, very few of the positions identified above would be used exclusively for the purpose stated. Instead, an individual faculty member might be assigned 60% of his or her time to direct instruction, 20% to student counseling, and 20% to service activities. In other words, the methodology being described is intended to provide a way to calculate the total number of faculty positions allocated to the college or department. Decisions on how each position is actually assigned will be made by the college and department administrators in consultation with individual faculty members.

Using the four major categories listed above for identifying needed faculty positions, the coordinator responsible for developing the allocation model must identify factors and relationships that can be used to calculate the needed faculty positions in each category and discipline.

To do so, he or she would review the long-range plan, discuss policy issues with appropriate administrators, consider available data that might provide typical average position needs, and prepare a written document describing the method of calculation and rationale used. The result might appear as follows. The figures shown approximate those used in a state-supported public university.

Allocation methodology for faculty positions

1. Instructional positions : # = estimated student/credit-hours divided by an average faculty productivity factor by student level and discipline.

Instructional faculty positions are calculated using estimates of student-credit-hour loads in each discipline and applying productivity factors by level for each discipline. Productivity factors are derived by specifying instructional modes (e.g., lecture, laboratory, case method) by level for every class offered in the institution and by identifying an acceptable class size for each mode of instruction. Productivity factors change slightly each year due to changing patterns of course offerings. Typical productivity factors are shown in Table 1. Student/credit hours shown per position correspond to the average number of credit hours produced during the fall, spring, and summer semesters by a faculty member who is employed full time throughout the academic year and summer semester and who theoretically is assigned solely to instruction.

Table 1: Instructional Faculty Productivity Factors

Annual student/credit-hours per full-time position employed fall, spring, and summer semesters and assigned solely to instruction (by level)

College & Discipline	Lower Level	Upper Level	Graduate Level
Arts & Sciences			
Biol Science	1397	899	594
Communications	800	1150	487
Computer Science	1507	1284	619
Fine Arts	1147	743	319
Foreign Language	1089	1067	637
Letters	920	1136	657
Math & Statistics	1120	1120	605
Physical Science	1298	886	440
Psychology	3712	1364	522
Public Affairs	1740	1397	789
Social Science	3020	1422	613
Business Administration	1392	1408	641
Education	1392	1218	732
Engineering	1557	1028	536
Health	1086	701	616

2.   Counseling positions : # = One full-time faculty position for every 400 student majors in the department or discipline.

Faculty positions are needed and assigned for academic counseling. This allocation is made on the basis of the equivalent of one faculty position for every 400 student majors officially enrolled in the department or discipline. In other words, it is assumed theoretically that a faculty member assigned **solely to counseling** could advise 400 student majors throughout the year.

3. Faculty activities positions : # = One full-time faculty position for every 11 faculty positions allocated for instruction.

Faculty positions are needed and assigned to accomplish creative activity, research, curriculum development, and public service. This allocation is made on the basis of one faculty member for every 11 faculty members allocated for instruction without regard to discipline or level of instruction. Stated differently, this allocation assumes that the institution can devote slightly less than 10% of its faculty resources to research, creative activities, and service.

4. Academic administration positions : # = One full-time faculty position for every 15 faculty positions generated in instruction, counseling, and faculty activities combined.

Faculty positions are needed and assigned for the purpose of providing academic administration and faculty governance. This allocation is made on the basis of one faculty position for every 15 positions generated for instruction, counseling, and faculty activities combined, and identifies faculty positions that can be devoted to administrative tasks. In actual practice, few faculty positions will be devoted solely to academic administration, but when all partial assignments are added together, the total is expected to be approximately the number calculated in this category for the department or other budgetary unit.

This example of an allocation model for faculty positions is one of many options that could be expected to evolve in a college or university. Factors that emerge as important will depend on the history of the institution, constraints that may be placed on the institution by the governing board, and on the goals and objectives outlined in the institutional long-range plan. The model identifies clearly the planned use of the resources being allocated and permits an immediate calculation of the number of faculty positions to be allocated once the expected student/credit-hour loads in each program or discipline are known. The model is easily administered using minimal computing capability and permits estimates of future year allocations if the information is needed. Perceived inadequacies in the model are discussed during the mid-year lull, when the pressure to allocate resources is not the primary issue. Such discussions center on improvements in the methodology of the model rather than on the actual resources to be allocated or received. Finally, the procedure is consistent from year to year, since the changes in the model are gradual and have limited impact over the short term.

Example 2: The allocation of operating expenses

Factors that determine the need for operating expense funds can often be identified using expenditure data from prior years. Discussions and decisions by administrators should center on the identification of broad categories of needs requiring operating expense funding and on the question of whether such funding is needed uniformly across disciplines or is discipline-dependent. Broad categories might include instructional supplies, travel costs, communications (telephone, postage), and the cost of service contracts on equipment.

An example of an operating expense allocation model is described below. Note that most categories are broad and make use of highly aggregated average costs in setting the allocation parameters. This model is used by the office of academic affairs at a major university.

The expense categories described below refer to the allocation of operating expenses needed in academic colleges and departments. Other categories would be needed to describe operating expense requirements in areas such as general administration, the registrar's office and student affairs.

1.   Instructional operating costs: Funding = $600 per full-time equivalent faculty position.

This category includes the costs of telephone, paper, pencils, photocopying, and other general needs in college and departmental offices.

2.   Professional travel: Funding = $750 per full-time equivalent faculty position.

This category includes the funds utilized to offset all or part of faculty travel costs to professional meetings. The amount allocated per faculty member is intended to be an average expenditure. The amount actually available to an individual faculty member will depend on policies established in the colleges and departments.

3.   Instructional travel and meals: Funding = $7 per off-campus student credit hour

These funds are utilized to pay the cost of travel and meals for those faculty who teach courses at a location away from the main campus. The calculation provides an average funding level for off-campus instructional activity. It is based on historical experience and the projected off-campus effort in the year for which the allocation is made.

4.   Discipline-dependent workload: Funding = $5 per weighted student credit hour. (See following Table 2 for factors.)

These funds are utilized to purchase class-related expendable supplies and to repair and maintain existing equipment. The workload weighting factors are shown in Table 2. The factors reflect significant differences in the need for expendable supplies among disciplines, departments and colleges.

Table 2: Examples of workload weighting factors

Discipline	Student Credit Hours Weighting Factor
Arts & Sciences	
Biol Science	1.00
Communications	0.40
Computer Science	0.70
Fine Arts	0.75
Foreign Language	0.01
Letters	0.05
Math & Statistics	0.10
Physical Science	0.90
Psychology	0.50
Public Affairs	0.01
Social Science	0.05
Business Administration	0.20
Education	0.20
Engineering	0.70
Health	0.70

This operating expense allocation model is one of many that might evolve following discussions with academic deans and department chairs. Noticeably missing from the list of expense categories is the cost of mainframe computing if these costs are charged back to departments. Note that each category used in the allocation model reflects an actual use of operating expense funds. This procedure gives the model credibility with both administrators and faculty.

The discipline-dependent workload category is the most difficult to establish and often requires keen judgment. This is also the category which is likely to change most rapidly. The workload weighting factors are multiplied by the total student credit hour production anticipated in each discipline to obtain weighted student credit hours. In this model, the disciplines of foreign language and public affairs are considered to have minimal needs for class-related expendable supplies. Biological sciences, on the other hand, is known to need laboratory supplies and chemicals, all of which are expendable and must be replaced each year. In addition, the biological sciences department has many items of equipment which require maintenance and repairs. The workload weighting factor in business administration is an example of one that has changed significantly in recent years. This discipline has placed heavy emphasis on computing and now must purchase software and maintain computing equipment for use by faculty and students.

The operating expense model is structured to permit calculations using a personal computer. Input data consists of student-hour estimates and the number of faculty positions in each discipline. If the faculty allocation model described previously has been used to calculate the number of faculty positions, the operating expense calculation can be programmed to run automatically from the faculty allocation model.

Example 3: The allocation of faculty salary funding

The allocation of salary funding for faculty positions is a sensitive issue and one that is usually highly constrained. In colleges and universities, salary dollar constraints may be imposed by the board of trustees, the legislature, the board of regents, a faculty union, and state statutes. In addition, campus administrators will wish to recognize cost-of-living increases, merit, and marketplace conditions. The formulation of a rigorous and quantitative procedure may be difficult, but systematic procedures can be identified and are described in the following paragraphs.

At least three factors are important in allocating faculty salary resources.

- College deans and department chairs must have some flexibility to recognize outstanding faculty performance through merit salary increases.
- The retention of top faculty members is essential for the continued strength and academic growth of the institution. It requires the payment of nationally competitive salaries.
- The recruitment of quality faculty is essential to the strength and academic growth of the institution. It requires that nationally competitive new-hire salaries be paid.

Faculty salaries are highly dependent on discipline. It is no longer unusual to find average salaries in some disciplines that are twice the average salaries in other disciplines. The same can be said of average new-hire salaries. These differences need to be recognized in the salary allocation policy.

The policy for allocating salary funding is often further complicated by the existing status of faculty salaries at the institution. Because salary administration is difficult and sensitive, salary increases tend to be equalized each year across disciplines. As a result, disciplines experiencing significant average salary increases in the national marketplace are often found to be lagging behind locally, while those that are static nationally have a relative advantage. It is not surprising that disciplines lagging behind locally are, when compared to the national salary averages, also the ones in which faculty members are in demand and mobile. The institution is clearly in danger of losing the best faculty in these disciplines and may be unable to compete for quality replacements.

If the institution is to maintain a competitive position, particularly in those disciplines that have high student demand and which pay high average faculty salaries nationally, the salary administration policy must reflect the national marketplace, and differential discipline salary increases will be mandatory. Administrators must find ways to minimize the disruptive aspects of a differential salary increase policy by making the rationale for the policy and the data supporting the policy widely known and understood.

A faculty salary allocation procedure that recognizes discipline differences and variations in the national marketplace is described in the following paragraphs.

1. Current faculty salary status at the institution

Existing institutional faculty salaries will be a matter of record and should be summarized in a table showing discipline and rank information. The second column in Table 3 provides an abbreviated and hypothetical example of the needed data.

2. Comparison of existing faculty salaries to national or regional data for comparable institutions

National data is available from several sources such as the American Association of University Professors (AAUP), the American Association of State Colleges and Universities (AASCU), and the Oklahoma State University Faculty Salary Survey. Alternatively, an independent study of comparable institutions can provide the needed data. This information is utilized to provide comparisons with existing institutional salaries. The third column in Table 3 summarizes the comparative data for this example.

Table 3: Comparison of institutional and national salary data

Discipline	Institutional number of faculty	National salary total	Average salary (total)	Percentage above (below) national average
Discipline A				
Instructor	2	$ 38,000	$ 39,824	(4.58)
Assistant Professor	6	154,812	163,806	(5.49)
Associate Professor	5	143,210	162,855	(12.06)
Professor	4	141,016	150,200	(6.11)
Total		$ 477,038	$ 516,685	(7.67)
Discipline B				
Instructor	1	$ 21,320	$ 21,000	1.52
Assistant Professor	5	167,830	160,995	4.25
Associate Professor	6	225,072	222,526	1.14
Professor	4	210,192	207,360	1.37
Total		$ 624,414	$ 611,881	2.05
Discipline C				
Instructor	3	$ 54,714	$ 52,000	5.22
Assistant Professor	8	198,264	194,720	1.82
Associate Professor	10	271,200	280,290	(3.24)
Professor	12	493,056	537,744	(8.31)
Total		$1,017,234	$1,064,754	(4.46)
Institutional Total		$2,118,686	$2,193,320	(3.40)

3.   The allocation of salary dollars

As the data in Table 3 show, Discipline B is in the best position relative to the national marketplace. Assuming there are no specific administrative reasons for this variation, available salary increase funding should be distributed to correct or partially correct the observed differences compared to the marketplace. A procedure for making the needed adjustment follows. The assumption is made that an average salary increase of 5% is available.

a) Across-the-board or cost of living increase

Allocating part of the available salary increase dollars uniformly to faculty in each discipline may be required by faculty union negotiations or viewed as appropriate by institutional administrators. In this example, it is assumed that approximately one-half (2.5% of the current salary base) of the available increase in salary funding will be allocated for across-the-board or cost of living increases. The calculation is shown in Table 4 under the heading Salary Increase Funding — Fixed.

b) Merit salary increase

Institutional administrators need to have flexibility to reward meritorious service and the achievement of the objectives outlined in the long-range plan. For the purposes of this example, it is assumed that 2% of the base salary total in each discipline will be used for merit increases. The calculation is shown in Table 4.

c) Marketplace salary adjustment

Table 3 provides the basis for allocating the remaining half of 1% of the base salary total in all disciplines if marketplace competitiveness is viewed as an institutional priority. One alternative would be to allocate none of the marketplace adjustment to Discipline B and distribute the funds instead to Disciplines A and C. The distribution to Disciplines A and C should be based on the relative differences between the institutional salaries paid in these disciplines and those paid in the marketplace. Table 4 shows the approximate result of this alternative but retains the 5% average increase in Discipline C.

The salary allocation described in this limited example will move Discipline A to a slightly more competitive position in the national marketplace, adjust Discipline B to a slightly less competitive position, and hold Discipline C at the same competitive level relative to the national average salaries. The tradeoff represents one of many difficult decisions that beset the budget allocation process. Table 5 (on the next page) summarizes the changes in relative marketplace position that would occur using this example. The change is small, but if the procedure is used consistently each year, the goal of maintaining competitiveness in the national marketplace among the disciplines represented at the institution will be achieved.

Table 4: Distribution of salary increase funding (example)

Discipline	Salary Total	Fixed 2.5%	Merit 2%	Marketplace 0.5%	Percent Increase Total
Discipline A	477,038	11,926	9,541	5,507	5.65
Discipline B	624,414	15,610	12,488	-0-	4.50
Discipline C	1,017,234	25,431	20,345	5,086	5.00
Total	$2,118,686	52,967	42,374	10,593	5.00

Table 5: Changes in relative marketplace position (example)

Discipline	Percent above (below) national marketplace before salary increases	Percent above (below) national marketplace after salary increases
Discipline A	(7.67)	(7.01)
Discipline B	2.05	1.56
Discipline C	(4.46)	(4.46)

ABOUT THE AUTHORS

Robert Cornesky is a Total Quality Management (TQM) leader in higher education. He was one of the first people to establish the principles of TQM in the management of a large unit within a comprehensive university. He is the principal author of the book that pioneered TQM in higher education, *Using Deming to Improve Quality in Colleges and Universities*. Cornesky has published several articles and three additional TQM books: *Implementing Total Quality Management in Higher Education* (with McCool, S., Byrnes, L. and Weber, R.), *The Quality Teacher: Implementing Total Quality in the Classroom* (with Byrnes, L. and Byrnes, M.), and *The Quality Professor: Implementing TQM in the Classroom*. He has over 25 years of experience in higher education. In addition to being a professor, he has served as the dean of a school of science, management & technologies at a comprehensive state university and as the dean of a school of allied health at a health sciences center. Cornesky has conducted TQM workshops for over 100 institutions of higher education, and is widely recognized as a speaker and educational consultant on all aspects of TQM in higher education.

Sam McCool is a faculty member at Miami Dade Community College, where he is taking technology into the classroom in order to create an environment for a continuous quality improvement theme. McCool has over five years of teaching experience and several years of administrative experience in higher education. He has taught beginning and advanced composition courses in traditional and competency-based academic programs, has been active in curriculum development and professional development programs, and has served as a consultant to business. He is one of the co-authors of *Using Deming to Improve Quality in Colleges and Universities* and *Implementing Total Quality Management in Higher Education*.